Daydreams

&

Lost Wishes

A Poetic Reveries Poetry Anthology

To the poetry community of Instagram, for making this anthology possible.

Table of Contents

Lost Wishes 177

Contributors   383

Foreword

Towards the end of 2019, four poets met in an engagement group and decided to come together to create a community on Instagram, one that focused on helping to promote new and upcoming poets. We devised a name—Poetic Reveries—and, from there, the page was created.

Many months down the line, we hit 20k followers, and set ourselves a goal—if and when we reached 50k, we would publish an anthology of poems created by the community. And here we are.

Daydreams and Lost Wishes brings together work from writers around the world and the Poetic Reveries team is honoured to showcase their exceptional writing. The Instagram community is a special one and deserves to be celebrated.

We're thankful to the poetry community for allowing us to hit the milestone and develop this anthology. Many thanks to all who submitted writing towards this project. We hope you enjoy this collection of your fellow writer's work.

Poetic Reveries

Daydreams

Of day dreams and lost wishes

I've been day dreaming for far too long.
Dreaming of what we could be,
Dreaming of what we were meant to be.
But my dreams were lost between tears and reality.
The reality that we weren't meant to be.
If wishes were horses, I'd rather wish for my happiness.
Because every time I wished for yours,
I lost a piece of my happiness each time.
I don't want to lose my sanity.
I don't want to break my heart again.
Because each time I wish for love,
I lose a part of my soul.
I don't want to lose my happiness anymore.
I want to feel loved again.
I'd rather not wish for anything,
Than live with broken dreams and lost wishes.

Kimberley Sasha Coutinho

Fade

streetlamps hum out into the darkness
illuminating all the glittering-gold lies
as the warm spring evening came along with first wild promises

my heart navigates towards
this unexpected kaleidoscope of emotions
that spill out to form life's new normal

the lights grow more lustrous
as the earth falters from the sun,
pursuing you in eternal graceless circles
against delphinium-blue skies

as five years struggle on my lips
and that first opal kiss dissolves
until we form the same breath,
these long-held perceptions of endearment
cascade quickly and fade

right back into warm obscurity
like an uninvited guest

Amy Laessle-Morgan

Stardust on a Summer's Eve

When I was little, I dreamt of you,
That perfect person, who could love me,
and make me feel warm.
Whose smile would light up my heart like the sun.
I dreamt, wished for that person who could save me,
and then I met you.
You, who taught me, guided me and whole heartedly
completed me.
You, who saw me, who noticed every freckle, blemish,
impurity,
and celebrated it like stardust on a summer's eve.
You, who made me see, the person I dreamt for, wished for, was
me.

Kerryanne Brown

<u>Hymn</u>

sometimes
life seems to
compose the
sweetest melody
just for me

every note
so beautiful
that it brings
me to my
knees

Laura Lewis

New Destination

I had a dream
It was to sing
I loved to hear my vocals ring
Upon the stage performers beamed
Living an exquisite dream
I felt the music deep inside
My passion for music shone

My soul stood on the stage with full blown pride
Until I realized I was becoming a clone
The performers all laughed and spoke the same
I was turning into a person I didn't recognize
Competitions became daily games
The animosity became prevalent in our group
How low was I willing to scoop?
Too exhausting were my days
I began to lose touch with my dream
I made a decision to change my ways
And find a new destination to happiness

Brittany Benko

Daydreaming of Australia

You can often catch me daydreaming
On a grey and rainy day
Dreaming of the life I could've had
In a land far, far away

With warm and friendly locals
And a laid-back vibe to boot
The quality of life alluring
Oh how I wished to put down roots

With frangipanis blooming
And sunshine almost every day
Outdoor living the way of life
A dream balance of work and play

Such stunning natural beauty
Coastal paths with heart-stopping views
One-of-a-kind wildlife enchant
But, alas, my visa was refused

Although my dreams were shattered
I'll always be grateful to Oz
For the memories I made there
My forever home that nearly was.

Helen C Green

"A Sweet Mistake"

I'm halfway in between my daydreams.
She's somewhere sitting on a cloud,
where sunny rays never shined so bright.
The moonlight sits in plight & every star has fallen from the sky.
The sour oceans have run dry.
I'll love her, even when the sun has risen from the west.
I gave the best of all my yesterdays to her.
Today is just another day.
Tomorrow's but a hopeless memory waiting in the winds.
I don't know how or even where I should begin.
I've swallowed pride from off my narrow tongue.
The sparrow seeks the dove once more.
My lips are bound to all her secrets, never known.
She's more than just a trophy girl to place on top a shelf.
I'd rather hide her from the world and keep her to myself.
I just don't want to be a selfish lover.
These selfless acts of love are often misconstrued.
We've missed the mark too many times.
We lost our wishes to the, "I love you's" and sweet "forget me
not's".
Forgetfulness is nothing more than just a sweet mistake.
So how can I forget a love like her's?

Jonathan James

Missing

It's on days like these

When I miss you the most

Your wonderful intoxicating scent

How my feelings it did invoke

The way you lightly tickled my neck

Inviting me in to join your dance

As lightning bugs merrily played

Shining upon this lovely romance

I could sit with you for hours

Until the amber rays kissed goodnight

Then sleep amongst the twinkling stars

Until Sunday morning rays shine bright

K.Wolf

King of Macedonia

By the meanders of Macedonia,

there was once a king.

Mountains and oceans,

stared at his might.

I was once a king,

with castles and armies,

and alone in my turquoise halls,

I reigned over all.

Chariots driven by unicorns,

merchants with gold,

All the world had to offer,

within my grasp!

A hollow heart,

Barren by sentiments,

My passion for power

was towering and unmatched,

But no one could define me,

A definition by one's love.

Daydreams & Lost Wishes

I was once a king who could conquer all

but oneself.

Love came once,

in the form of a fairy,

An innocent goddess,

fiery and passionate,

Loving me in my glory,

and entangled in my weakness.

Love is an illusion,

where everything appears seamless.

But true love is empty,

An illusion hidden in tragedy.

Her delicate mortality,

laid bloodied and bare.

I was a foolish mortal,

whom once sought to defy destiny,

But the embers of treason

slowly burned my empire.

I watched its ruin

from the chairs of my power.

Daydreams & Lost Wishes

I remember my reckoning

As the fire grew from the horizon,

I sat on my throne,

The flames of life burning a new dawn.

I was stirred from my dream,

to be comforted in my own tears!

Marx.K

Tin man

There were words,
words unsaid she longed for.
And like the tin man,
she stood immobilized, waiting for someone to save her.
She followed golden brick roads to satin curtains of deceit
and swallowed poison promises of healing.
And it was here,
she finally decided to listen to the distant echo inside her rusty
heart.
It was here,
where her very own beautiful unsaid words were hidden.
And it was then,
she realized; the oil can wasn't really out of reach after all.

Debie Collins

The Lost Cloud

I sat back with the windows down,
Listening to a tune.
Nowhere to go but just letting the mind flow.
I watched as the clouds roamed.
One cloud kind of looked like you.
I suddenly heard your giggle beside me,
I couldn't believe it was true.

You suddenly grabbed my hand.
We got out of the car,
And started to dance
Like we used to.
As cars passed by,
You were not at all shy.
You did your silly moves,
While I covered my eyes,
Laughing hysterically out of embarrassment,
Hoping no one would see you,
But hoping that you'll never stop too.

I laughed so much that tears flowed from my eyes,
I wiped them away,
Then you were gone,
Without a trace.
I realized,
I was still sitting in my car,
Listening to a tune,
Thinking of me and you,
With tears falling down my face,
Wishing that you stayed.

Abigail Alvarado

Evasion

From the rattles of world
I try to find refuge
in the solitude of my soul
I evade getting touched by
the harsh winter
that chases me
my heart seeks
a warm vibrant spring
amidst the freezing ghettoes
lucent dreams carve
a hazy arc
from the horizon of yesterday
I remember a
different version of myself
through the summer boulevard
I try to get away from my present
on a quest to get back to my past
but the cycle goes on....
and so does the life.

Ali Ashhar

My Darling,
Once upon a time…
I ruled over an icy frozen kingdom, destined to topple under my wicked power into utter doom.
You ruled over a faerie wonderland amidst the enchantment of spring, destined to bloom.

Our kingdoms were connected by a third in between.
There, it was the autumn of September where we encountered each other, two polar opposite queens.

It was you, the beloved Faerie Queen that was adored, enchanting everyone with your beauty and compassion.
Leaving a trail of blossoming roses and daisies in your glorious path.

It was I, the Frostbitten Queen, who everyone despised.
Leaving a trail of sparkly ice, while blowing a tantalizing winter breath, so they ran in fear of my wrath.

Yet, I secretly gazed as you and your friends entered the room, while everyone fawned over you.
Your laughter, purely melodious, a harp can't compare.
For a brief moment, my icebound ears turned warm, it's true.
Ravishing smile and you radiated green, pink and purple hues.

French pink dahlia petaled dress, sun kissed skin and floaty chocolate hair.
Who wouldn't stare?
You were the Goddess of Spring and Happiness, no one could bear to see you in despair.

Your friends couldn't compare.
They were troublesome, I was aware.
Hearts forged from ironware.
Amidst that circle of iron hearts, you were the diamond,
solitaire.

Alas, who was I to warn you amidst your reverie of a daydream?
With their iron hearts and my fearlessness, how could I be
responsible for a possible bloodstream?
How could I obliterate from your glowing face, the sun beam?
I'd let time itself be the Timekeeper, so in due time you would
see through their scheme.

Your cheerful being didn't deserve to be cursed by me, so I put
away my grimoire.
I admired you from afar.
Back in my kingdom, after you, I named a star.

Despite our circumstances, destiny allowed us to meet.
But it was not our time to be together yet.

I could never accept your friends and they could never accept
me.
And this Queen doesn't plea.

Even though we could meet in this sacred kingdom.
I was destined to my kingdom of cold doom.
You were destined to your kingdom of spring bloom.

I was drowning in the winter storm, tears of frozen waterfalls all
night.
Icy winter abyss, no ray of light to shine it bright.

You were in a state of euphoria, spreading roses to everyone all day.
A life full of colour, never grey.

I was experiencing sadness, anger, dismay, and vengeance.
I needed to learn the friendlessness and loneliness of winter, in order to anticipate the era of spring and cherish it like a prayer, without ever taking it for granted.
I needed to reflect on my being and my life beneath the crescent midnight moon to make way for the sunrise and prepare mentally and emotionally to seize the day without wasting a second.

You needed to experience the bounty of loving others, nurturing them like tulips and never taking them for granted because after your season of spring, even the most lovely tulips will wither away in winter.
You needed to live a blissful, worry free, ambitious day beneath the blazing sun, before experiencing the confusion, sadness and haunting thoughts being provoked underneath the dark sky with but a shining moon.

It was not our time yet.
But it is now…

Now, I can be my true self and cherish you completely.
Now, I know I've earned you like candy, so sweetly.
Now, you can be near me without fright.
Now, you can lean on me and set your sadness and pain free.

This is our time…
No longer a crime…

Nighttime or daytime…
Wintertime or springtime…
Forevermore in this lifetime…
and until death reunites us once more in heaven…

Alina Hamid

To this day

To this day

I still remember those walks through the market with my grandmother,

where she would tell me all those stories about witches,

spells and potions

when we passed in front of the herbalist's stall

which I always watched in slow motion.

We always did the same route

as I stayed outside when she entered the fish market,

eating an ice cream while she talked with the older women.

Whenever I cried at any moment, she was the only person who didn't tell me "be a man".

She wiped my eyes saying: "it shows that you are a Pisces".

To this day

I still go to the same place to buy my favorite bottle of eucalyptus honey

and think of her every time I blow the candles for my birthday

although she's missing and I miss how she used to caress my ears and kiss my front.

To this day

I still wonder where will go

all those wishes that we ask for

and that never come to pass

I would have liked to see my desire come true

to see her a little more time

sunbathing on the surface from her towel

while I greeted her from the sea

swimming with my little feet so as not to sink.

How she took her crushed magazine out of her bag and read through her sunglasses.

To this day

we continue to care for her garden in the hope that any tree planted will be a living memorial of great longevity.

And that wherever she is, when the wind caresses its leaves, she feels us close and remembers us.

We're putting in all our effort, trying to never kill those plants that we water with the oceans of tears we cry

every time we think of her.

To this day

I still make a wish

every 4th of March

without knowing if one day

it will come true.

Marc Francesc

Songs of spring foregone

Melancholy reminders of summer's end deepen

Champagne clouds in scarlet skies

Here comes the last rain of the season;

As winter breaths on my neck

Lost in my turquoise wonder

I hear;

Songs of the dying leaves

I see;

Trees and their feathered dreams

I breathe;

Smell of new soaked earth

And new beginnings

With my sun kissed dreamy eyes

I have seen all there is to life.

Now more than ever

seems it rich to die.

Parul Shanker

<u>Evaporate</u>

Let me be
the drop
of rain
on your cheek.

Let me be
the one that
rolls down
your skin,
absorbed gently
by your pores.

Let the rest of me
mingle in with
the textile of
your clothes.
Hugging the dust
on your lips,
embracing you
as I evaporate.

S.A. Quinox

"Truth of love"

Agonizing in self-love,
I feel my heart is adamant to cajole itself.

Dreams are only replicas of what we really want,
Yet the sound of truthfulness is an unfaithful breeze of unspoken
desires,
Where the spikes of heartbreak gels in every heart.

Soothe the heartbreak of my beloved,
Since love is adamant to cajole itself,
With an abundance of self-love.

Alshaad Kara

Midnight Song

Dancing light of lost crepuscular rays
crossing velvety aurora displays,
What remains in the shades of November
Vestigial blush ephemerally lay.

The queen of sunsets' poetic sonder
ignites prosaic woe into wonder,
The siren's song gently in the abyss,
pleading for each darkness to be kinder.

Until then, the quantum of silence speaks,
Tearful through the eclipse of midnight's kiss,
Tightly wrapped in a bittersweet embrace
Till secrets and the full moon coexist.

Painting all her daydreams and lost wishes
through these eyes of intangible canvas,
The rhythm of the heart is mapped in verses
for one more midnight's kiss on moonlit scars.

Jaime Boey

<u>Open Window</u>

I've lost myself in kitchen sinks
in unmade beds, on unswept floors
my eyes have glazed
my hands fall idle
stopped mid-dish, the water cools
lost in thought, in battles fought
in what could? what if? how and why?
a breadcrumb trail of never was
the sinking stones of wishes thrown.

Ahead, the open window calls me
worlds await beyond these walls
this box, this cell, this house
no home, a place where
dreaming went to die
where love lay faded, far forgotten
choked in dust and bitter ash
all the dreams we had long lost
a love too small and now outgrown.

We shared the air that filled these rooms
but life inside could not sustain

outside the green fields
beckon softly, I must look
beyond this pane
the curtain gently falls and flutters
shafts of sunlight pierce the bars
my heart beats, my lungs expand
I breathe fresh air to call my own.

Amanda Waldron

Be(little)

What shall one do on a night when the January cold casts its
frosting breath?
What shall one do on a bleak day to temporarily assuage the
frostbites underneath the heart's depth?
What shall one do in predawn hours, when one's eerie
phantoms lurk to haunt, yet one bears no mental strength?

Woefully, we mortals subconsciously know the answer.
In these times, we unlock the magical door beneath the waves
of our souls like a dancer.
To reminisce as a coping mechanism and to return to the only
place where we can be a prancer.

Behold, it is our long-forgotten innocence,
a strewn oddment that completes our soul,
that bedazzles us as a whole,
which awakens during these times of solace,
even if it is equal to that of an obolus,
to melodiously coax us into past reveries,
with memories that were such treasuries.

A past place known as, "childhood days,"
when we were drunken-dazed,
with a nebulous gaze.

When little things we ignored,
are now considered "too old,"
but, are truly what we now hope for.

41

Much like when we were asked, "How are you?"
and were able to say, "Great!" without a compulsive thought's
review.

Much like when we used to receive a warm pat on the back,
for completing a minor task,
which are now so rare, that we are placed in a state of bask.

Much like when we used to write about the things that once
caused us to beam with smiles,
in diaries that are now long gone or stored far away in hidden
piles.

Much like when we read fairy tales and we knew,
that no matter what anyone told us, in our hearts they were
true.

Much like spending Sunday mornings, playing with our
favorite toys,
Now an obsolete ritual because, "We're too old and they make
too much noise."

Much like going to the park and having thousands of races
and hysterically laughing on the ground with our messy ice
cream faces.

Much like running around, giggling at each other's silly jokes
and remarks,
but then again, that was the only time our eyes had illuminated
fiery sparks.

Much like when we used to rhapsodically shout out dreams,
which would change every week,

like an old habit,
but these days we have forgotten them and can no longer
revisit.

Much like when we were upset over a stolen cookie,
looking for this "sadnesses" cure,
only to gaze at the night skies from afar,
imaginatively wishing upon a star,
cheekily laughing, like a magnificent lyre,
and instantly forgetting what made us ire.

Much like when we were still but a child,
which was also then our latent inner child,
the only fragmented part of our true essence, so perfectly wild.

Oh, how those were our carefree days of youth,
like the home that we long moved out from, yet where our
mind still wanders to.
Oh, how life took an unforeseen turn,
Yet, we still reminisce on the shared past, hoping to return.

*It was these little things that allowed us to be(little), unknowingly
gifting us the tiny, chrome droplets of love,
but today, these same little things are the ones we be(little), in order to
grow up, and in a closet, shove.*

Alina Hamid

Creating Young Manifestations
from Lost Wishes and Daydreams

Reminiscing about the days when I was younger,
Being a dreamer filled with so many
Hopes and dreams –
The time when
I believed in
The magic of
Wish granters.

I entrusted my hopes and dreams
Unto the kind, fluffy dandelion flowers
And then I watched
As the seeds of my wishes
Drifted away.
Not just that.
I also wished upon
Lucky clovers, birthday candles,
And airplanes resembling shooting stars at night –
Believing that doing all of this
Would make my dreams come true.

I waited.
I waited patiently as I gazed up at the clouds,
Daydreaming my future.

However,
With my future and where I am at today,
I later realized

Daydreams & Lost Wishes

What one would eventually realize . . .
Though I wished upon make-believe fantasies,
To have believed felt so great and wonderful.

Though everything might seem
Like lost wishes and daydreams,
I would like to think that everything I did
Was what I would like to call
"Creating young manifestations."
All so honest, innocent, and filled with bliss.
True to my heart
And still
Remaining
A part of me.

With all my beautiful
Manifestations of my past
And all my beautiful
Manifestations of my present,
Each day,
I am looking forward to seeing
How far my manifestations will take me.
Whether it would be beyond the galaxy
Or simply small skips by the river,
I will embrace each step gladly.

Angelica Lyanna N. Garcia

Where the Darkness Takes Me

Wednesday tendencies and overcast eyes.
Tea parties adorned with scissorhands and darkened daydreams;
blackened tulips and cups not made for everyone.
Beautiful and delicate and macabre.
A place where the wind hauntingly strokes wisps of my hair
and everlasting labyrinths call my name.
Indeed that's what I set my heart upon as a little girl.

Ann Marie Eleazer

Ghost Ship

Living through this half a life

Through smokes and mirrors of unsaid dread

In this time of restless, stubborn whims

Do I wish I could choose you instead

Of the tattered sails of this empty ship

With the putrid smell of broken vows

I know our paths must disunite

Across these seas, but tell me how?

Nah…

My questions best kept sealed with me

Inside my bones and witless quips

Mayhaps you will still remain

In cracks of my soul and nervous ticks

And as I steer on through this murky dark

Placid tempered unraging storm

From ashes to ashes and dust to dust

Forever searching a shore to belong

Avin

Surviving the Dream

Everyday, we

fight against time and ourselves,

for our fantasies.

Kathryn Holeton

A Somnolent Night

Day dreaming of the wished
That tides against the shorelines
A day so fine
Let me dream a little more
For what I wished for
Had already come and gone
So let me dream a little more
Children got swept by the sea
Let me dream a little more
Planktons dancing unseen
Let me dream a little more
Stars twinkling in the shadow
At lost for words
So let me dream just a little more
Be mantling my dream
All over the non-oily tile
These overly timed somnolences
Come and go
All the burning Stars
Waking me like wine
So I could be somnolent again.

Najaree Ratanajiajaroen

<u>Dollhouse Dreams</u>

Once upon a time
I was a little girl filled with glee.
I would use all of my dolls
To act out a family.
I would create storylines
Mirroring my dreams
Of people loving one another
To block out any screams.
Years passed by
And everything enraged her.
Dolls put in totes under the bed;
Too much turmoil in the head of a teenager.
The dreams of family disappeared
From emotional abuse.
Her hopes shattered so often,
She figured there was no use.
College years came around
As the flames grew hotter.
Simple eighteen-year-old actions
Led them to not need a daughter.
Hopping from couch to couch
Taught her family was a lie.
So many sleepless nights;
She ran out of tears to cry.
Her friends had saved her life,
But one stood out from the crowd.
His bright smile shined;
His personality loud.
Much to my surprise

He too had jagged edges.
Life was not handed to him;
He too had scaled ledges.
I fell for him hard,
Like Barbie loved Ken.
I dreamed these days
Would not reach an end.
Time has brought us
Love and a marriage.
Life feels like I'm a queen
Arriving in my carriage.
For years I feared family,
But with you that has changed.
All my harmful past views
Have been rearranged.
Now I let myself dream again;
I hope for a little girl.
I'll get her every doll she wants
And I'll give her the world.

Brandi Begin

I want to lay with you

I want to lay with you
In my bed
Under the blankets
Your arms around me
Holding me close
Our legs intertwined
A sensual play

My head on your chest
Hearing your heartbeat

Feeling my breath
So warm on your skin
Our hearts start beating as one
Our breathing in unison
This is intimacy
This is what I want
I just want to lay with you

Charlene Fox

You are tucked away
in the corner of my heart.
This way I will always
have you near —
in the momentum
of how you once were.
Madly in love and still spending
the passing of time with me.

berkana.vuno

<u>Wanting</u>

Oh how I want you
Want to feel your skin
beneath my fingers
Want you
to close your eyes
in the palm of my hand
Want you
to sigh against my lips
and inhale my whispered words
Oh how I want
to ease your troubles
and stir something new in you
Oh how I want you
And oh
how I want not to

Cate McMinn

Sacred Feminine

I often dream of transcending my skin,
shapeshifting into supernatural
creatures who are not me;
having unlimited powers,
like the oceanic allure of a siren,
or the tragic beauty of a fallen angel;
the burning, rebirthing resplendence
of a phoenix,
or the serpentine, primal magic of a goddess.

I want to express my *divine femininity* and be unashamed of it.

Charlotte Gébert

Frozen In The River Of Dreams

Frozen in the river of dreams
stood the ice queen, ripped at the seams.
The current, too strong a flow
too many destinies unknown.

With a toe dipped in each babbling brook,
she dabbled 'til she became too crook.
Weakened and wistful, she turned to the book.
Pages transpired as her pen overtook.
It was then, she remembered, she was a chef, not a cook.

At last, her frozen heart began to melt.
No longer fully numb, the more she felt.
No longer running from the tidal streams.
Now pacing across the stepping stones of dreams.

Chrissie Hyde

A Vernal Vision

Where branches are bridges and sedges are screens,
And waters reflect a celestial shine,
The earth makes a canvas and seeds are a means
To paint a terrain of Edenic design.

A labor of love attentively lays
The pedestals of an herbaceous surround:
A savorous haven that settles and sways
Once nectars and milkweeds emerge from the ground.

Within the embraces of petals and blades,
Sprinkles of delicate pearl stones are drawn.
They cluster in luster while under the shades,
And wait for the livening ardor of dawn.

These satiny structures then break from within;
A subtle subsidence exposes their cores,
And shimmers embellish the layers of skin
Of ravenous larvae that rise from the pores:

A subtle invasion, embodied in slinks
That fashion a hole in each foliaged hold,
Before manifesting, with sinewy links,
The tenuous tents of a crystalline mold.

Away from the host plants, a cycle of peaks
Blossoms on beds with a billowy blend;
A bounty of fragrance and succulent streaks
That beckons the chrysalis slumbers to end.

The butterflies waken and start to undo
The remnants and binds of their previous form.
They cling till their flickering wingspans accrue,
And hie to the heights in an opaline swarm.

They fluidly frolic and run on the breeze.
They brighten the glow of the greenery's gleam.
They tend to each stem and encircle the trees;
They nourish and flourish, and kindle a dream.

Daniel Moreschi

That old tree

With last light
    of a star gone dark
and memories push
    us further apart
into the cold, dark night
when the wind
         refuses to sing

You and I sit
      by that old tree
  looking at the eternity
frozen in a teardrop
  of the songs we refuse to sing

The silence aches
    with the unsaid verse
in a melody of
      notes unheard
An orchestra of
    the cosmic scale
  holds its breath
and then…   oh it's too late

The sky falls down
    in drops of gold and white
In a raging storm
      of blinding light
A symphony
    of destruction
      of our world

59

And we still sit
       by that old tree
till the ground gives away
       beneath our feet
and no one sings
       the songs unheard
         and no one cries
          and no one speaks…

Avin

All the intense passions I had have changed over the years.
Some fading into the background, some painting new broader
colors
Into my world that I thought was already quite colorful.
I was so sure of who I wanted to be in my younger years,
And almost all of it has changed.
We plan our greatest accomplishments and think we know best
only to find
That sometimes we weren't reaching high enough.
I know I wasn't.
Through all my missteps, disappointments, downright
dangerous times…
I still came out with a resiliency in my bones I never dared to
dream I had.
My dreams weren't lofty enough to climb the peaks I have
endured.
My boys are men now, and I am finding myself wishing again.
Who can I be now?
I'm learning that I can be much more
But I still don't dream high enough..

Dawn P. Harrell

Dandelion Dreams

I walk upon a bed of thorns.
My days drained as I bleed
oxidized yesterdays.
I wait for the bandage of tomorrow
and the universal promise of time
to heal me.
And when darkness spreads its cloak,
I fall upon a bed of dandelions,
waiting for the god of wishes
to dust my dreams
with pillow promises.
This hope that I rest upon
Keeps me alive.

Debie Collins

The Scary Lady and me

Scary is the lady before my eyes,

Made my heart beat three times in an instant.

Taught this fool to dream, filled my mind with lies,

Made it plan for a future so distant.

In two-months' time, I'll give her a present.

Within one year, she'll have to see me too.

After two years, my feelings ill present,

And in seven years' time, she'll say I do.

Truly dreadful even without her spells.

Just sat, spoke, smiled ever unconcerned,

Shared screeching silence 'til she bid farewell.

With this, my daydreams to lost wishes turned.

Now my heart longs for the next ride, next dance.

For the next chapter, next juncture, next chance.

Delton John M. Go

A Letter to Daydreams

To my daydreams of purple and pink,

You hold me captive in a wondrous world of wonder that
doesn't exist
You feed me on elixir and ambrosia and give me wings of
crystal blue
You kiss my pains the sweetest goodbye and hug my icy
melancholy warm
You love me. You love me right unlike the taste of love that
turns toxic overnight.
You know my heart and my inner child like I wish I could.
You have my hopes and dreams stacked in neat piles of wishes
to be granted.
You radiate bliss and beauty and make everything glow.
I almost always forget that you are only a dream, a dream too
good to be true.

- the child you never loved

Divya Singh

All the Words

If I were
a true poet
whose blood ran
black as raven feathers

If I could merely
bite a vessel
that bled
thick-running ink
whenever my words
clamored
for release

If I splashed out
my soul in lines
in weary words
upon the hungry page—

the first of those
would most surely
be you

    You
        You
            You

You   Because all the words
in this wide world
begin with—you

Dona McCormack

Daydreamer

I love to sit and daydream
Let my mind wander free
Think about the bigger picture
Places I'd like to see or be
Relaxing the soul
And stretching ones imagination.

Donna McCabe

<u>My Dream Within Dreams</u>

I was nurtured by a loving family
buried in a hibernaculum of hope
held in a myriad of young dreams
some of my stars died—some evolved
but two sacred reveries emerged

to grow and find myself ensconced
in my greatest of aspired dream
wrapped in a protected hermitage
of a lavender mountain sanctuary—
exalts a benediction beyond words

our small—warm sheltered home
where true love radiates between
the kitchen scents and the fireplace
breathing in its woodland of safety
electrifies my glows for a future

I often escape to ponder or write
and praise God for a divine family—
meekly raised in clear alpine airs
perched aside still humble waters—
I'm healed in nature's sentient grace

hand in hand with my dear wife—
lovers—we emerge sporadically
to drown our oldness in kindness
and smiles of our ever-growing
family and small-town friends

in this forest of a joyous fulfillment
she still turns our house into a home
and as I touch her perpetual touch
I feel an authentic refuge of warmth
for she is my one dream within
dreams

Doug W. Evans

<u>Longing</u>

After a long, dark, cold, sleepless night,
The sun began to peep, scattering its light.
Are you hiding in the rays that shone?
Are you shivering there, lonely and alone?

In my blinding haste, I didn't see,
The rush of the waves rolling along the sea.
Whirling winds, gushing, making noise.
Shhhh.. Did I hear your sweet, soft voice?

I sat on the road, exhausted with glistening tears,
People pass me by, with their clicking heels.
Did I just glimpse your smile among them?
I waited and searched, but none came.

I search for you in the rain, in the wind, in the waves,
In the forest, even in the lion's lair and caves,
Then among the chaos, I heard a guitar strum somewhere,
I clasped my heart, and listened well, you are there.

Raye Bautista Sy

That day on the
cliff of the North Sea
You made love to me
that moment with you
My favorite fractal
etched forever in my mind
A ripple in the fabric of time
When I close my eyes
for the last time
I will go back
to our tiny fragment
by the North Sea
So for eternity you
will be making love
with me

Carla Gagen

Love in Covet

I speak to you in silence

Whisper the song of the soul flows and airborne

Glide through the soaring breeze

Letting go ardent desires that ignite for you in flame

For the heart has surrendered and embraced your existence

Longing for your presence

Grieving for your love that wasn't heretofore

Virahela

A Dream

I wait.
Tucked in that space
Where longing
Feels safe.
Fallen to sunlight
And spun
Into gold.
Lost to a dream
That can never
Be told.

Emily R. Paget

Folklore and Fantasy

She is a study in
folklore and fantasy,
hidden behind
silver, storm-filled eyes
and her dreams
are filled with magic,
with a backdrop
of melancholic sighs

and you can find her
in the evening,
casting spells beneath
the waxing moon,
and hoping that
her wishes
will come true
very soon.

J. Sexton

Cover me as I rise

Cover me in sunset rays
your prismatic beauty display
Gloam away my flaws
Radiantly over grey
Charred scars of the past
from impassioned blaze,
My plea before you go, enfold
me in your fleeting glow

Have we grown accustomed to
the familiar sight of the horizon?
Building bridges in warm kisses
through the fate of wilderness
Lift each other out of darkness
as daydreams over lost wishes
and been through every weather
all the years on this path together

As deep as the roots of an oak tree
As versatile as bamboo in the face of tsunami
As wings take turns throughout the flight
The sound of bells fades in twilight
under the restless, sombre moon
silence envelops with empty words
barren sighs of winter's breath
incarcerate ill-fated remorse
duelling echoes of regrets
could this be a lifelong nemesis?

Songbirds to the Morning Star, harmonise

the void of hope interweaves a pathwise
Pollinating monochrome memories memorialise
but whispering death threatens to terrorise
a weakened soul's fatefully carburises
In the shadows, cover me in sunrise
stirring verse to my soul
and all of me with love
Cover me as I rise.

Jaime Boey

Desolate Dreams..

There was a wanton abandonment
To dance to the imperfect symmetry
Of the symphony of hope
After escaping the binds and shackles
Of those desolate dreams
Those footprints of faith
Kept me on the right path.

Donna McCabe

I see a little girl waiting outside the school
and watch her daydream
Her arms reaching wide
she tiptoes forward with long strides
through grass and small white flowers
Balancing for a moment on one foot
almost tipping over
before setting the next one down
Part of me wonders what's in her mind
Part of me remembers

Cate McMinn

"In my daydream"

I wish I could stop time
or make it last longer.
My eyes are filled with wonder
while my heart is floating like fire,
now I'm lost in a daydream.
A daydream—
forgotten in an instant,
almost
small remnants left behind.
A daydream—
where our best ideas are crafted,
when exhaustion takes over,
when second guessing yourself
is so exhausting that you don't even bother.
A daydream—
where the time skips at random intervals.
A daydream—
Where am I again?
I don't want to wake up.
I'm happy here.
I want to stay here,
in my daydream.

Precious Magdaleno

Daydreams

Daydreams of tomorrow
Moments
Captured in still time
Linger
Quietly in my soul
Memories
Yesterday's replays
Entwine my heart
With a teardrop symphony

With a nostalgic
Twist of fate
Today becomes yesterday
Reminding me of what was
A wish
A hope
A prayer

Today
Exploring the wonders
Of life's possibilities
Seizing wonderland's probability
Entwined
With love

Frolicking
With whimsy and fancy
Reflecting moments
Of life's serendipity

Guided
By your heart
Learning
To believe

Daydreams of tomorrow
Precious pearls
Of what is to be
Sprinkles of fairy dust
Engrained
Engraved
Magical memories
Treasured moments

Tammy Muehlfelder

"I WANT TO BELIEVE.'

I want to believe

In the journey,

Not only the destination.

I want to believe

In goodness,

Not rotting trepidation.

I want to believe

In the supernatural

And mythological creatures,

In psychics and magic

And the nature of preachers.

I want to believe

In an afterlife

That isn't Heaven or Hell…

In meditation,

Manifestations,

And a universe parallel.

I want to believe

In miracles,

And that equality

Will be achieved…

In loyalty,

Dedication

And that we get

The help needed

In a list of medications.

That demons and evil

Don't live inside of me

And that people

Only speak honestly.

I want to believe wishes

Made on falling stars

And that pinky promises

Are a sacred covenant

Of the heart.

I want to believe

In second chances

And story book romances

And that joyous moments

Outweigh the joyless.

But most of all

I really want to believe

That the purpose

Of this all

Isn't pointless.

Tessa Glasgow

HATE OR LOVE

—

Share with the world what you love. Don't let it disappear as you spend the short years of your life courting your hatred. You've already won it over. Hatred will show up at your door with a bouquet of thorns. Hatred will follow you around like an animal on the hunt. It will stay and stare and wait for you to fall. It will never give up. And you can keep watching your back

But there's *not enough time for that, my love.*

This life cannot be dedicated to hate as love becomes the quiet voice in the air. And though it, too, will always be there, it's faint whisper can only gather its strength if you give it the attention it deserves. Sing it with *praise* and let it *blaze and burn* brightly through the darkness. Let it become all-consuming until your light allows for new gardens to grow. Beautifully blooming in body, mind, and soul. Your life becoming the poetry and prose that's been spoken about for a century on silver screens and though some believe you don't need to romanticize every cup of coffee, I must ask them

Who told you to stop dreaming?

Life can be full of monotony in the day to day. It can be full of hatred as they prey on your insecurities and deem you unworthy as they twist your meanings. Speak out when you need but continue to believe that there is *magic* in living. Let your main focus be on the love that does exist in this world: your passion, your dreaming. Because *that is the life you need.* That is the life *waiting* for you. To hate or to love.

Which will you choose?

Jena P. August

84

freedom

It started with a slow drip.
An unremarkable trickle that crept under my words
tucking itself away behind my hesitations and often humble
declarations. I
ignored the tearing.
Raised the volume of your laughter over the ripping sounds so I
couldn't regard the cracks forming in my bearings.
It was the way you talked about her. A
steady shimmer that peeled atop your pupils like a sunrise and
a subtle drop in your shoulders while you uttered her name as if
settling into a warm embrace.
There was a weight in your voice. A
glaring heftiness that mocked the sheer hollowness that
accompanied your time with me.
Years of constructing monuments of my worth to you,
cleaving my way into your heart as I pretended not to see *her*
likeness carved into your chambers,
tethering my identity to your smiles in ways that didn't feel like
shackles, and still,
you rewarded me with emptiness that felt like *half of you.*
I noticed the pieces missing. More than half; rather,
notable chunks of you that lay scattered along her memories like
offerings. I
can hear the splitting now. That slow drip.
That bleeding wound seeping into my foundation
       has unraveled me.
Disentangled my existence and reduced me to a huddled mass
quivering at the hem of your robe as I gather the last bit of
strength I have to
free myself of the burden of attempting to love you better

than her.
I simply tire of being *good enough*.
I am weary of merely being *tolerable*. A
flavorless meal that is too bland where it should be savory;
despite the reality that I am a garden of sustenance
done with dying in her shadow.
Unbind me from what was lost to you.
See in me the light that burns for you because,
in my ill-fated attempts to have you
   in the ways that you'd merely permit,
I realize there is no light in you.

It still shines in her. Yet,
you search for wildflowers in your desolate fields
while forgetting to regard them blooming in me.
I do not exist in the past with you.
Soaking up the earnest rememberings of an immature love that
no longer serves your present.
   You are not him.
Stop seeking solace in brokenness and graveyards and
seek me for the mark my presence brings or
continue to die mourning your barren fields as I
finally find the one bold enough to simply
   love me back.

J. Lovelace

Another lost boy

I

Like all the other children that he knew,

he grew on stories told to him,

he never thought that they were true

yet always touching him within.

The story that was closest to his heart

was of a boy so far away,

a story where he longed to play a part,

a world in which he longed to always stay.

II

His da' would always tell him that

he had to keep his letters straight

and keep his bedding flat

and always wake before it's eight,

and never barefoot run outside

and make sure that his tie was tied

and always keep a sober stride –

pretend that he was grown, and not a child.

III

- His story told him otherwise

and he wished that he'd never grow;

for growing up came with a price

and he would gladly let that go.

His mother would berate him for his dream

and said he had to live within his reach,

that while his fairy-tales are good-and-gleam,

reality should be his only liege.

IV

With time he learned to keep his letters square

and banish to the night his dreams to fly.

He acted as is seen as proper; fair,

and slowly, slowly, Tinkerbell would die.

So when life's wonder would catch up to him

once in a while break through his thickened wall,

he'd harden heart and soul and limb,

and never answer wonder's call.

V

While wonder is hard to snuff out, make cold,

the boy with vigilance would guard his head.

So with a hardened heart the boy grew old

and left his dreams with other fancies dead.

He got a job, and wife, and child,

and scoffed at stories told by his dear wife:

would never let his heart grow wild –

he was an adult, with a job, a life.

VI

From stories of his childhood's magic spell

through tears they watched him from their secret grave,

t'was Wendy Darling, Pan, and Tinkerbell,

that after all these years tried to stay brave,

that one day he would see the flying boys

and whisper words he surely knew;

remembered through adulthood's noise:

that 'I believe' in pixie dust, and fairies too!

VII

But Wendy watched in agony

and Peter Pan, he faded behind bars.

And Tinkerbell cried rampantly

and pixie dust seemed further than the stars.

Though hope had lost them far, too far ago,

at times the old man smiled –

and through his eyes they saw him grow:

they saw their hope; they saw his little child.

VIII

With hope rekindled Peter Pan would fly;

and while the fairy gathered pixie dust,

the old man blankly stared – and he would cry –

He felt his heart with urgency adjust

when Peter Pan flew over to his son.

But though he felt a pang of loss, a chill,

he never realised what was done,

his heart was hardened to their magic, still.

IX

When Tinkerbell came to his son, she found

a boy whose mother nurtured wonderlust,

a boy where magic grew in fertile ground,

here she would sow and gather pixie dust!

And in the boy, their magic grew

and in no-time the boy had dreams to fly –

again the stories that they lived were true

again there was a sparkle in the eye.

X

So filled with joy was Tinkerbell and Pan

that soon their memories were blind

to who was once a boy but now a man

that left his sense of wonder far behind.

But Wendy, Wendy never could give up
but cried and waited patiently.

Though there is little hope when you've grown up,

She sits there still and hopes, belatedly.

Johannes Karlsson

"Sanctum of the heart"

In a daydream of love,
I was brought to heaven.

Hey Cupid,
Why did love choose me?

Among all the men I could fall in love with,
You chose my heart as your target!

If true love is meant to be,
Then sanctum my heartstrings as a sanctuary.

I shall be the passion in those vines,
A steadfast obsession in the journey of infatuation.

Among all the men I could fall in love with,
Love chose to bloom inside my heart...

This romance shall be enhanced with angelic petals,
Blessed from the heart,
And celebrated in sanctity.

Alshaad Kara

Senses of You

I cannot make you hear me, but these words seep from me with a burning lust to know every fibre of being that defines you.

Echoing within the storms of men in your life; ushering you into the sunlight, the warmth and the shelter that this forest can provide in the most fragile of moments.

I am here for you, if only you would hear me.

I cannot make you feel me, but these hands long to hold yours, clasping them in a protective shell as I deflect the evil, as I reflect the love. From my palm to your palm, I promise you protection.

A protection so powerful that I will form a shield around your soul with the layers of molten lava, that is this love of mine over the cracks of all the men that have come before and, with their Earthquakes, have broken the beauty within you, but this is our time now, I will protect you...

I reach on out to touch you, if only you could feel me.

I cannot make you see me, but I wait for your eyes to catch sight of mine, so we can redefine the definition of love at "insert number here" sight because, within the beauty of each other's eyes, I want us to keep on falling for each other for the rest of our days and, every time we gaze into each other's eyes, I want you to feel at home, at peace, at happiness, at done with all the fucking bullshit emotions that have destroyed you before because this is our time now and although I cannot promise you a life of eternal sunshine because the storms will come, I give you my word that I will be there, right by your side as we face the changes of weather together, however...

I cannot make you see me, but how I want you to see me.

Jonathan Young

The third dream

As an erudite sage once asked the perpetuator,

What is the only thing worthy of leaving a dream for?

Probably another stronger dream,

Or perhaps two.

But what if, by virtue of wanting the third,

You end up losing all three.

A misfortune of epic proportions,

Would look miniscule in comparison.

As a decade glides on and you introspect,

There was a technicality with an escape clause,

The second one was always accomplished.

The path that ensued with the choice,

Leads you back to the first dream,

Which in due course was perfectly executed.

And the third?

That is the whole problem,

The nub of everything you are,

Or ever were in continuum.

Karthik K Raichurkar

IMPOSSIBLE

It's easier to handle when the

impossibility is swirled with dreams and heights,

of wishes and grand wanting in nebulae of

imaginary worlds, so I

float,

knowing it will never be that good,

picturing it even better.

Katherine Cota MacDonald

When the living is easy

Waking up without an alarm clock is the pleasure of my generation.

Lying on my back, seeing how the pine trees cover the sky and the balcony awnings cut across it,

I realize that summer has already arrived.

And so the melted snow that I carry inside me makes me know.

The rocks bloom from the tide and, in the streets and houses, I can already see the surfinias, hanging the petunias and my eyes fill with life.

I feel that nothing that has happened has been in vain.

Now the living is easy, I take a look and he's next to me.

My flower is the jonquil and his gemstone is blue beryl.

Deep Blue Aquamarine.

It is no coincidence that his first love was the sea.

I am nothing but a sailor,

a writer,

in which you can easily navigate his words.

That's why he wears a sailor knot

bracelet on his ankle and I wear a ring

in the shape of a wave.

We both know that no matter what happens, we can always find each other here.

I am no longer young but, in my head, I will

always imagine you drinking a tequila sunrise

in the same place, no matter how much time passes.

Because daydreaming drinking sea breeze cocktails

is the nectar of the gods of the generation

in which I have had to live in.

Marc Francesc

<u>Chimeric dreams</u>

Dream, my love.
Closely out of reach.
Vague but crystal clear.
Come to me, come I beseech!
For my arms long to hold you in,
And my heart lurches for you from within.
Yet your frame lives like an illusion,
Ensconced in where my
Loveless lovers stay,
Untouched.
Where they speak like a dream,
Laugh, cry, like a dream,
Walk, rest like a dream,
Breathe like a dream.
Where they live,
And forever
Reside.

Karen Chan

<u>Bigger Fish to Fry</u>

Old dreams flit into my head
under the natural spotlight
that floats in the sky.

Oh, the ideas I used to have,
a teacher, a princess, a witch–
All the things I was told
wouldn't come true,
that I should set free
into the abyssal ocean.

As day transitions to night,
I abandon
all the fantastical dreams
from a younger time,
reality is calling me back…
and I have bigger fish to fry.

Kathryn Holeton

"You Can't Dream If You Don't Sleep"

bedroom air the color of midnight

i dance with the shadows

of people who live in my memory

my body is a ghost town

i sit alone on beige sheets

quilted blanket at the foot

the only thing haunting me

is sleepless nights

melting candle wax

long stalks in wine bottles

dim glow like warm stars

paper town— just burn it already

Kelly Riddle

Into The Wishing Well:

His caustic blue eyes were menacingly dark as he perched himself on the old wooden bench. He leaned in close to me while the seat creaked under his shift in weight. "And ya know what aye had seen?" His thick accent clung to his words, dragging each syllable from his soft palate, as if he were pulling sentences from the back of his throat with a string. He took a drag from his cigarette, and sucked on the butt with his lips, as if he were kissing his wife. He blew the smoke to the side and placed his arm on the back of the bench. He smiled. I shifted in my seat; my knees knocked together awkwardly. He noticed. "Aye said, ya know what aye saw?" I shrugged. He inched closer. I held my breath. "The stone boulders on the side of the hill sing. Its voice whistles through a triton shaped crack, and if ya listen closely now, you can hear it through endless stretching groves." He paused, and waited. I listened. There was silence. "If ya can squeeze yer way through— the boulders I mean — inside the hill, there is a place called the Faery Well. No water resides there. Flames that ignite hotter than a bubbling cauldron claw up the sides, hoping the faint of heart are tempted to tumble in. But, if yer brave enough to extinguish the flames, the hollow bones of the spirits call out to ya as a last effort, before your own demons rise. And just when ya think the worst, ya won. And yer free." I tilted my head to the side, furrowing my brow. "Free?" "Free." He confirmed. "From what?" "From the human world."

Kiera Gold

Dream Life

Do you ever envision your dream life? I can see mine so clearly.
I wake up early to catch the sunrise, hot coffee in hand. Lush
greenery surrounds me and a view of the not-so-distant ocean.
When the wind blows you can smell the sea.

Little yellow house

By the sea ever so blue

Basking in sunlight.

I tend to the orange trees in the yard and have fresh mint
growing in the entryway. My rescue dog sits close by. Pretty
soon, he'll bark as the cows walk by for their morning exercise.
Later, as the sun sets, my love will return from a long day at
work. His arms envelop me and our lips meet. Everything else
melts away.

Can you see my dream?

Peace, quiet, simplicity

And a love that lasts.

Lindsay Peckham

Salty souls

In any season of the year, in my head, I always try to be on these hot and sunny days where the weather and the hours don't matter, without much to do apart from breathing fresh air.

Just having radiant eyes and sun-dyed blonde hair.

I was beginning to wonder if this feeling was ever going to arrive.

The one you get when you return from bathing in the sea and the water from the shower runs through your body as if it were a silken Milky Way.

When you see the shopkeeper from the corner, early in the morning, place the cup of coffee on the hood of his recently parked car.

The first dip of the day, which freezes your body but fills your soul. The first song that comes to mind when you dive into that exact moment.

When it's always a good time to write your thoughts on paper and redeem yourself.

I am a daydreamer.

My soul is made of water and salt. And I know I'm not the only one.

One day, I am going to wake up and it will be September: back to school, routine and work.

But I won't feel alone, I'll keep daydreaming. I will know there are more souls like mine, who are among us

and live in an eternal summer time.

Marc Francesc

UNDER THE GRIEVING MOON

To the world, he's the perfect picture,

Loved, respected and wholesome.

To me, he feels like home.

I have a safe place, in my mind.

A meadow lounges by a river,

At midnight,

Under the velvety sky,

While the stars are running wild with all their might.

My night sky,

Guarded by a loving moon

Who sings my soul to rest

With her sweet caresses and tunes.

Enchanting me with his eyes full of stars and moonbeams,

Comforting me with his delightful laughs,

Exciting me with his teasing touches,

Serenading me with the most endearing lullabies,

Companying me through tough times with wise advices,

Enveloping me in his warm embraces,

He has become my safe place.

But the world wants him.

A part of him,

Some parts of him,

All of him.

And I also want him.

I want to be a part of his world.

I want him to be a part of my world.

He visits me at my meadow again,

At midnight.

His hair floats in the summer breezes.

His face lifts up to the sky, contently.

His eyes close, peacefully.

He loves this place, dearly.

Like how I adore him, faithfully.

But the world seeks for him.

The cruel, harsh world

Who only asks, takes, and possesses.

They keep reaching for him

Who only answers, gives and shares.

One look at him and I know,

It's time I let him go.

Keeping him by my side,

I have no power for such task.

Pushing him back to where he belongs,

My heart breaks beyond repair.

Trapping us both in this fantasy,

All we have left will solely be despair.

One look at me and he knows,

I am about to let him go.

His eyes soften, sadden and become clouded,

But the sky above us is crystal clear?

His smile strains, fades and seem burdened,

But the stars are still harmonizing their cheers?

So I force a smile, and nod,

My vision blurred, my soul fractured.

His forehead touches mine, tentatively.

His eyes once again search for my eyes,

Sorrowfully.

He understands, and I understand,

What we have is more than what the world can fathom.

He remembers, and I remember,

How much we both love this memory, the melody and the
river.

He sees me, and I see him,

We see the hidden broken parts.

We see the fragility.

We see our true identities.

He kisses me, and I kiss him.

Our last kiss, under the grieving moon.

This haven will lose its glow soon,

And the songs will sound greatly mournful.

But he knows me, like how I know him.

And when our eyes meet,

In this final moment,

I can scent the fresh grass,

I can feel the soft ground,

I can hear our secret song,

I can see my night sky,

I can see his smile, bright as starlight.

Meadow Z

"Dream of Wishes and Wish for Dreams"

I dream of wishes, and wish for dreams,

Of happiness and pain.

I dream of a life worth living,

With all its sunshine and rain.

And life could make my soul at ease,

Where I can lay down on gentle pastures.

For what else could I hope for,

To be at peace, ever after.

After what little life I've had

Has gutted me, and left me out to dry –

And love has given me a bitter taste,

And no more desire to try.

So I will lay down to dream, and think of things

That would make my heart beat faster.

For even when I sleep, I wish,

For that life worth chasing after.

Melanie Simangan

The Joker

Do I dare alter His fair design,
or is amour above all divine?
For bound she be as I here behold,
yet I undress a body's story told.
Why here, why now, and in this way,
another card in fate's cunning play.
A Queen to King, but joker me—
wild and changing to make matches curiosity.
How in me should she place some trust
when I change faces like the politically just?
Quick and cunning shall I win her heart,
steal the game; force the court to part.
And what our thoughts have done, our flesh may do—
until another card is dealt. The Joker, the fool.

Michael Bruan

watch me drown

in the sea of light

rippling in your eyes

watch me fight

to breathe in an air

mixed with your redolence

watch me surrender

to your tide of love

and your wind of adorance

watch me re-float

onto your golden skin

and lose myself on this

beach familiar and akin

watch me rise

watch me collapse

watch me heal

watch me relapse

into a love like deterioration

like an illness without medication

watch me sober up

then watch me drink

from your lips then beg

"I'm addicted, don't you think?"

~visions~

Mohamad Allouch

The Way Deities Want

I too, find bliss in loneliness.

To be alone and cry tearless –

Free to daydream and make-believe,

Free to flee, leave the life I live.

Crowds of crowned clowns exhaust me so.

Sensing their non-sense trashy shows,

Preaching matters that don't matter,

Feeling unfulfilling after.

But, I too, in lonesome wonder,

Wish – pray, to be beside me, her –

The lone jester I see serious,

The one I dream 'til unconscious.

My grand wish will stay in daydreams.

That's the way deities want it seems.

For me to live and die alone,

For her to be candle unblown.

Delton John M. Go

nowhere

this poem is a call.

unanswered by humankind.

this poem was born out of a dream.

undreamt by our ancestors.

this poem leads to *nowhere*.

to a place in our hearts, our souls, and our minds.

to a truth that hasn't become our truth - *yet*.

our ancestors dreamt of a land beyond the ocean - their nowhere became truth.

our ancestors dreamt of a society in which women could vote - their nowhere became truth.

our ancestors dreamt of the abolition of slavery- their nowhere became truth.

our ancestors dreamt of a nation not divided by a wall - their nowhere became truth.

our ancestors dreamt of flying to the stars - their nowhere became truth.

and nowhere continues to become the truth.

because someone is *brave enough*

to believe,

to imagine,

to dream,

to speak out,

to start being the change.

so, let's believe in a peaceful world.

let's imagine justice always wins.

let's dream about a society showing love and compassion for each other and the planet.

and then, let's speak out loudly.

let's use our words, music, and art to make our neighbors dream the same dream.

eventually, we will be the change we want to see.

eventually, we will arrive in nowhere.

eventually, we will be the ancestors

who believed,

who imagined,

who dreamt,

who spoke out,

who started being the change.

and we will find, our wishes lost have always only been a dream away.

Navina Donata Baur

Brave

Someday, I will be brave enough

to build a castle in the sky.

The one we dreamt of,

you and I.

One day, I will have the courage

to spread my wings and fly

Into the Heavens

without you by my side.

Nicole Carlyon

Countdown

What use is there in counting years
when we have dreams?
I take no stalk of the imaginary
but harvest the ashes of each season,
planting their lessons and reaping vision,
an oracle and her garden,
learning to live.

The stars ask me
to write the stories of their constellations,
for they are unsure if they have ever slept,
and night avows to hold the best tales,
ones in which regret cannot beget
withering grey,
nor wrinkles of the tongue.

I will plant, I will write,
so that this repository of hope
never becomes a reliquary of dreams,
within it a sorrow
which can no longer be spun into gold,
ever listening
to the ticking of a clock.
    -   ohm

Oksana Maskulka

Utopia

Half awake and half asleep,

I walked along the paths of fields,

Like silent sonnets of velvet dreams,

Where you and I used to be.

We ran

In the fields

Of mocha woods and cocoa clouds,

Echoed in the forests a wildflower's song

Where flutes of forever

Painted pastel promises

Of silver and gold.

You filled my eyes with Solomon skies

as my poetic mind rioted

those delirious desires.

I opened with a sigh

my teary eyes

but in this full of darkness,

you were nowhere to be found.

Perhaps they were scattered recollections of reality

Of this time last year

And written in the stars,

A forgotten name I remembered.

As everyday, in my sequestered longings,

I wrote letters in an invisible ink.

I think I knew

Your heart couldn't be reached;

What I have left with me

are my dreams of a Utopian life

in frozen vines of time

where hope dances dangerously.

You will live forever with me.

Parul Shanker

LIGHTHOUSE

—

Lighthouse levitating from the ground underneath
Or so it seems to a disoriented sailor
Praying he can reach
Is it a mirage or a dream
The wind is singing it's disastrous song
The light soon dims
Now long forgotten
Kaleidoscope skies as he lays on his side and the waves carry him
away
His face now dusted with stars as the dark cloud pulls his boat
out from under him
He clings to the waves but a feeling of peace alleviates his pain
He believes he's back in Maine
Sipping a beer on his porch
Watching the summer rain
He pats his old dog and stands with a smile on his face to greet
his family
Finally, they cry
Levitating
Waiting to bring him home

Jena P. August

Paracosm

To the girl that I am yet to call my home,

Hello, it is so nice to finally meet you.

In person, yet I feel I have known you all my life.

Your words have become my oxygen,

When you left the first time, in losing you I couldn't breathe.

But from your voyage you returned, and from the richness of your lips I found myself clasping to every breath, every word and every meaning to keep these lungs of mine,

Inhaling

You, my safe haven.

He whispers, I will be there to love you.

Then I exhale as I clasp your hands as together we are safe, protected, and as I lose myself so willingly in the oceans of your eyes, yearning to discover the depths of your soul, I want to uncover you, and discover the lands for which you call your own.

I want you to feel safe enough in my arms to be vulnerable, to unravel your soul and unwind the strings of your heart for which have many ballads of both joy and heartbreak, and play them to me,

I will listen, intently, and if I was to be so lucky to be invited in, I would compose upon your heart so intricately that we would be woven together like patchwork and ours could beat together as one, I would frame your soul like artwork so deep within

124

every fibre of my being that, to break you, the nightmares of life would quite literally have to tear you from my flesh and bone, set me ablaze and filter you from my ashes.

Yet still your happiness would not be found to be destroyed as I would carry it so deep within my spirit that we would transcend time and space as we know it to be.

In this paracosm of a world written by me, I will continue to tell stories of the journeys of the blue eyed lady and me.

But if ever your love should arrive,

Welcome home.

Jonathan Young

High Heels & Cloaks

And when the daydreams didn't take me,
the darkness always did.
A hand-in-hand sort of love affair
between my mind and soul,
atop castles and tree tops,
dressed in high heels and cloaks.
Where the day couldn't reach me, but the night took my oath.
How sweet, when reality takes a backseat
and the fantasies take me home.

Ann Marie Eleazer

"Hello there, stranger."

Hello there, stranger.

You are the light and the shadow,

You are either here nor there.

I remembered the first time

my heart smiled at you—

such a lovely daydream,

my mind may not always

remember exactly what happened

but my heart will always

remember the feeling.

But you drown me unexpectedly

after you draw these lines,

broken lines— all so clear.

I trusted you

not to destroy me,

I'm vulnerable

but still you did it,

unforgettable.

Now, I'm giving

myself time

to let you go,

so I can be

at peace

to my shattered

Pieces.

Precious Magdaleno

DREAM

Tiny as Little Thumb,

Eager and sparkling,

A messy girl

in her dreamy world

With shaggy hair,

Has crazy affair

With the bubbles,

Tumbling in puzzles

Of jiggling mind.

She lives in creamy

mists of warm clouds,

That carry her

like Aladdin's mat

Into the school of magic,

Where

Time flies in white horses,

Stars enjoy carnivals

Of Moon & sun's unison

Against the horizon,

Alike saffron brush

dipped in crimson hues,

Rabbits take shapes

Of clouds,

Deers jump upon

thunders,

Unicorns sprinkle water

with their horns,

Penguins blow snow

with their mouths,

Dragonflies with

colourful arms

Carry her

Through darkest tunnels,

Where fireflies welcome,

To touch her up

With golden attire

And pink blushes

from woody flowers

& sanguine sky;

And her messy hair

dressed by peacocks,

Like Rapunzel's.

Ephemeral like shadows,

The magic of her fantasies

Are piled up as sheets

In miles and miles of poetries;

A place that's safe to hide

The magic she broods,

Which she refuses to share

With her own reality.

Bubbles clang

In abode of blues,

She loses the cloud

Of her dreams

Like Cinderella's heel.

Lost and confused,

When morning glitter

and her dead clock

Wake her up;

No more fireflies,

No more clouds,

No more rabbits,

Her puffed pillows

Drag her lazy;

She carries herself

To the mirror

And she finds herself

In a deserted island,

With brimming thoughts

echoing loneliness

And no one true enough

to share her dreams.

Priyasha Panda

Garlands of Grief And Sorrow

If I had a time machine by my side,

I would have been to the past,

Looking at the September rains in my heart,

And finding you beside the garden.

Letting you go was not only a pain,

But also shocking, as I forgot to breathe

And calm myself down.

Beneath those scars, there was a little melancholy among us.

Thinking of you, I walked upon the cobblestone streets,

Your images surrounded my subconscious mind,

While sleeping under the cherry blossom trees,

The soul sank, but my heart clasped in mixed feelings.

I saw some strange dreams come true,

Beneath the cerulean skies and falling rafflesia,

Sapphire and selenium was what I deserved from you,

But you were standing near my grave of sorrows.

Daydreams & Lost Wishes

I wanted to ask you some questions,

Will you watch the leaves start falling, the way you fell for me?

Or do you want to see me at least once more?

Let me know before the moon laments for you.

Not so long ago, I lost you in my own void,

But found you watching the stars in the north,

Because colors have their own story,

And mine was a rainbow combination.

My voice sang songs of desperation,

And some words from the poetry of remembrance,

My grave was bleeding with the ink of wounds,

There lies beneath it, the garlands of love and grief.

The sea swept me to its Rock bottom,

So do not stand there and wait for me,

I will soon be gone above the clouds,

Where you will never see me again.

Reon Sylvester D Cunha

Daydreams & Lost Wishes

Where the sun never sets,

let's disappear there,

embraced by the

silence of twilight,

it's now or never,

our daydreams & lost wishes,

awakened under soft curves

of hazy, violet breaths,

mingling sweet summertime,

strawberries,

and full moon kisses,

that can't be still

or rushed,

our skin pressed

and sweaty,

heavy and high tempo,

holding each other

as unbreakable,

where we are free,

it's our paradise,

135

bodies together like an

eternal blushing night,

continuously melting

under sapphire skies,

glowing,

between

daylight's

lingering shiver.

Wilder Rose

Please

The moon halos upon my shoulders.
Her milk drips from my wrists.

Come here. Sit with me.
Look how I pulled her
from the heavens.

Indulge yourself with me.
Drink her honey from my palms.
Drink me from yours, before I crust upon your flesh.

I cannot root a home with you.
You know very well, I am temporary.

Come sit with me, before I drop to my knees and vanish into
a perpetual new moon night.

Please, just sit.

S.A. Quinox

Chasing Rainbows

Forever chasing rainbows

Of my dreams, ambitions and goals

Knowing they will complete me.

Donna McCabe

<u>untitled</u>

a thumbnail moon,
a speck of light.
a void.
duality.

pearls of sweat
form round my neck,
breathlessness
and
mortality.

if i can ascend
the depths of this unease,
i will quench my thirst with the sun.

i will watch her light
drain from her face,
and i will know that It has won.

Kelsey Singh

Flute Song

I heard the roving balloon man

from mellow sound of flute;

which he, full aggrouped in a bag,

would pipe about his route.

I heard him warbling varyied sounds,

with palms woody and roon;

his tips, through notes, fiddled with ease--

reprising tune to tune.

I heard his clomps, when treading nigh

the home with roughy ground;

from sloshings knew, his turn about

the boggy marsh around.

I heard his songs meander there,

through countryside and quartz;

the children in wee socks and shoes,

did on his music, waltz.

I heard the tunings, dim and faint--

when fields, he'd rambling go;

no ploddings of his boots were heard,

so of his bimbling toe.

'Twas childhood joy, now long foregone,

its mirth I lived before;

and yet, his fluting, peals in me,

tho' he is heard no more.

Shamik Banerjee

An evening

She sits by the window at dusk,

each day,

watching the golden sunset,

settle speckles of sparks,

on her house.

She smiles with anticipation.

The darker it gets outside,

the brighter her house glows.

And she sees them!

Her two daughters in their nightgowns,

running around the house,

giggling, glowing.

And her love, looking at her,

with a radiant smile.

That of two proud parents,

marveling at the wonders they've created.

Her heart warms up.

But why isn't she with them?

She moves towards the couch,

to her world,

but tiny sparks have turned into fiery flames,

she can see the curtain vanishing in flare,

but she ignores it and keeps walking,

the floor is scorching,

but she must hurry.

There they are smiling at her,

their faces golden,

their bodies ablaze.

Why isn't she with them?

She falls to her knees,

to her pyre,

but it all vanishes in a flash.

All gone,

except the cold.

It's dark and freezing.

She's alone,

as she's been since the accident.

Why wasn't she with them that day?

She thinks, as she curls up,

longing for some warmth,

in this freezing hell.

Sonal Bains

CITRINE DREAMS UNMEASURED

Your beryl troubled seas
found my sail without a name.
Ravaged heart and wrecked dreams
swathed in ruinous sable shame.
Trapped under those layers
from my vacuous lilac gaze,
you wiped away my tears;
rekindled dreams of fuchsia days.
Empty words no more,
we treaded silver haunting pleasure
Soaring over rainbows
winged on citrine dreams unmeasured.
Passion bled its sins
under ruby skies of lust.
Stars witnessed our win
as noir nights rolled into rust.
In pressed petal flush
you were longingly baptized,
as brick upon brick
I built my home, within your eyes.

Stuti Sinha

Starlight Wish

Crystal fears
Jagged and broken
Lifeless and still
Reflections and refractions
Of love's cast asides
Lost wishes
For all we've dreamed
Heartfelt goodbyes
To all we've forgotten
Along the way

Hopes we've endured
Reflected in yesterday's moments
But lost in today's darkened imagery
Loneliness spreading her wings
Encasing the heart
In jaded 'what could have beens'

Moonlight reflections

Shadows of what was

Recreated memories

Yet to transform

Yet to reappear

Nighttime shadows

Fading with dawn's grandiose
Hope on the horizon
Showcasing gleams of promise

Heartbeats of Tomorrow

Illuminating and transforming

A glimmer

Of starlight wish

Tammy Muehlfelder

Between burgundy and mistletoe

She hurried down the avenue,
head down to shield against the snow,
wrapped in a coat coloured in hue
'tween burgundy and mistletoe.
       Snowflakes whirled in the wind
       by the streetlights they dimmed.

Something was hidden in her eyes
that peeked through lifted hand and hair;
she carried something of the skies
– by that short glance I lost cohere.
       So the ground became white
       and a mirror of light.

When I that evening went to sleep,
I could not shake that image fair
of eyes that were – a trope – but deep.
I, mortal, charm'd without compare.
       Outside my bedroom walls,
       snow in darkness still falls.

The very next day, I returned
to make my new delusion real:
that in this lifetime: mortal; spurned,
an angel could be mine to feel.
       The snow turned into rain
       with a wistful refrain.

Johannes Karlsson

"IF I COULD WALK INTO MY DREAMS."

If I could walk

Into my dreams,

I'd take with me

When I return from sleep…

The solitude

That hangs strewn,

Somewhere between

The stars and moon.

The pain free

Version of me

That adventures carelessly

To destinations

Far from reach.

The imagination it takes

To unconsciously create

The utopian landscapes

Of artistic escape.

The weightlessness

Of a gravity free reality,

And all the possibilities

When nothing anchors me

To human disability.

The freedom and release

From manmade obligations

And unrealistic expectations,

And everything that comes

With forging

My own aspirations.

The fearlessness and gallantry

Afforded to me,

Unwaveringly,

In place of hesitation

And groundless insecurities.

But most importantly,

I'd take with me

The recollections

Of my yesterdays,

So the memories

Never fade away

With the inevitable decay

Of my aging brain.

Tessa Glasgow

Meditative Stitch

The long weekend's
meditative stitch,
summon my inner Zen
for each threading ache
to forget my nervous prick
causing irritating itch;

To sew a straight line,
undeniably a chore.
Oops, the obvious glitch
makes a frustrating flaw;

I wonder if I could switch
for an easier fix,
but I couldn't sleep.
It's a little girl's hope
to create her own,
a heart-earned masterpiece
called Batu Seremban;

Repetitively, she fills
her daydreams and lost wishes,
unseen tears and silent fears,
gathered to be stitched
tightly into tiny pieces;

She knew that she would
share her handmade with love,
and they will come to know
what she's made of.

Jaime Boey

<u>Songs of Seasons</u>

I've been awkwardly
sliding through life for
all the years I can recall.
Now investing time and training
into this passage process –
I'll persevere with perfecting
a gracious gliding motion.
The symphonic sounds of
the autumn winds shall
sing me through these seasons –
and I shall mark each one anew –
feeling it with fresh eyes
and a sage heart.

Tiffany O'Brien

PORCH STEPS

I sit on my porch steps,

Engrossed in watching

The tangerine sky above me.

What a wonderful sight!

Ah, some wonders these day-dreams are too,

Popping out of nowhere,

Empty yet so fulfilling.

And, here I go again,

Dreaming of building a home

On the horizon,

With you by my side

* * *

I sit on my porch steps,

Catching homeless words

Floating in the wind,

Waiting to be crafted

Into a beautiful, meaningful poetic garland.

But, alas, they weigh heavy in my hand

Reminding me of all the poems

I've written for you

That you never got a chance to read.

And so, with a sigh,

I release them into the air again.

* * *

I sit on my porch steps,

Sipping ginger tea,

Thinking of you again.

Or maybe, I am awaiting some sign

From the universe

To tell me to move on,

And to assure me

That I am fine,

That I am sane,

That I am immune

To the insane ways of this world

* * *

I sit on my porch steps,

Lost in time,

Drowning in regret,

Living in empty dreams...

Vandana Pamulaparthy

Impulse

refractory beams of sunlight spilt like seawater
through trees desolate fingers
I remember how the air of that moment hanged heavy when
dilating iris' counted clockwork orange impulses
penetrated the fundamental elements
of our own human nature

I want to reach up to meet your hands
once again entangled with mine
we are the very work of art that
allowed us to detach from one another
as these shattered moments spill out
onto this forest of free reign

Amy Laessle-Morgan

THE REAL YOU

If they knew the real, you could they deal with you? Ask yourself honestly, could they cover you? Your scars & unhealed wounds that leak blood every time you think of the past & moments that never last. You kept the memories & most of the time, you & old your old friends had a blast. Stop & ask yourself. What if they knew the real you? Would they love you instead of abuse you? Would they actually take the time to know you? Instead of use you. Like how you enjoy the simple things in life but don't mind the finer things. Like how you reflect on the past good times & the joy it brings those moment that made your heart skip a beat. Now you know why the caged bird sings. Ask yourself, do you know the real you or is it all a dream....?

Willandria Jackson

Living in a daydream,

or

not all wishes are lost.

Stars fall, make a wish.

How pathetic.

Dreams,

The worst kind of masochism.

Break and reassemble

your poor soul, self – destruction.

For how long?

Until she makes a decision,

She doesn't want it anymore.

Until death.

There is no dreamland, where all wishes come true,

where streets are paved with pink love,

and the air smells like fresh cotton blue.

Pie in the sky,

just psychotic illusions,

of incompetent clowns.

The mind is obsessively possessed with self-delusions.

Will he justify his tragedy,

his useless existence,

with awkward kind of comedy?

There are no rainbow bubbles

which protect you.

Only reality,

a grey wasteland of futility

shrouded in freezing mist.

A cacophonic symphony of clenching teeth and fists.

Rotten leaves falling into a black river of bloody tears.

Kingdom of nightmares,

where his Majesty of vanity abuses the Princess of humanity.

Star falls, make a last wish.

Close your eyes and be the clown, allow yourself to dream.

Even nothing is always something.

For it happened before, the poor incompetent clown became a King.

Zuzana Gmucova

between worlds

I dredge the husk
of dawn's silkened light

I am here, yet not here
a visitor in two worlds
the door, a latticework of eyelids

horses, ephemeral in lash lit pitch
saunter past
their tails catch the dark canvas
beckoning

submerging

the meadow of my dream
washed
in soft lavender sorrow,
blinks

aching

and the call of amber sounds.
shattering
this votive wombscape

I ooze
hollow through
the moth's transparent wing

I am born

Jai Michelle

<u>Another Life</u>

Comfort, love and freedom,
What I yearn for as I sit gazing,
Clear pictures surround me,
As I stare out of blurred eyes.
Caged in a glass mansion,
My heart hurts for the fresh air
Upon my face,
And the sizzling sun
Against my skin.
Chaos rules here,
Underneath the tone of riches.
Spike shards of glass line the hallways
Of the smooth shining outer walls.
Dreaming, cold and unsettled,
As people pray at my feet,
I long for Golden dragonflies,
To show me how to fly away.

Kerryanne Brown

Be Careful What You Wish For

Wishes often send us down rabbit holes
where madness and wet lips await.
We cast pennies as little girls
and spells as women and witches alike.
I've learned we must be careful what we ask for,
especially in the middle of the night.
Because they are always listening…
the crows
the moon
her light
her bite.

Ann Marie Eleazer

Memories

Here I lay, within a field of awaking purple hyacinths,
chrysanthemums and daffodils.
The rays of sunlight waltzing all around.
Let me reminisce…for memories are all I have.

Memories of a time when we were naively engrossed within
our youth,
the hands of Time had yet to move,
frolicking down hills, hands intertwined for ring around a rosy,
sipping away to our treasured drinks.
Squeaky laughter all around, sleeping oh so sound.
Daydreaming dreams of togetherness, foreverness.
*Will I remember this time again? Will I still be struck with a whiff
of nostalgia from the things we loved in childhood?*

Memories of the times to be locked away into the abyss,
forcefully forgotten.
Shrieking horns of wars,
needles and swords,
stabbed directly towards,
what was never ever yours.
*Can I ever throw away these blazing oars of anguish, instead of
holding on to the aches like a fool?*

Memories of changes, loathed joy.
Tsunami of tears, racing down a youthful face from departure,
what could be more harsher?
Dazed in a peculiar place, with peculiar people, doing peculiar
things, am I the imposter?
But there I discovered my cheerful marchers.

Marching me towards the golden gates of a spectacular scenery
that is only ours.
Will I ever accept this unmarked? Will these treasures remain with
me forever?

Memories of blurs.
Days racing Time himself,
quicker and quicker,
but what changes?
Same routine on replay each day,
blurry haze, drunker dazed.
On a sunny day, will I ever ponder upon these blurs? Will they ever
have meaning?

Memories of home and family.
Home like a palace, kingdoms away.
Time, he's the wanted foe.
Family living out their lives, so different from mine.
Joy and joy, but never there are we.
Until destiny decides.
To when, there is nothing but utter contentment,
endless nights of gazing upon the stars at twilight,
conversing because when will this time come again?
Just don't let me leave.
Will we ever return home? Will I ever see a room full of smiles
again? Will we ever be reunited without being faraway?

Yes.
And yes.
But yes.

These are merely memories.
Memories I'll hold dear, until the time is near.

Daydreams & Lost Wishes

These memories, don't let them vanish in thin air.
For memories is all I'll ever have...*forever*...in this world.

The bygone friends that remain as a memory, never to be seen
in this world ever again,
The family I wish was with me for all of eternity...

Death isn't what does us a part,
awake from its eternal slumber,
and it's what reunites us,
forevermore,
in a heavenly place.

Alina Hamid

<u>To Sing</u>

My heart is ready to explode
in the colours of the setting sun
in hues of the bright and the bleak
in shadows of my dreams that I seek…

The weight of the world that I carry
would not part ways with the strife
through the harrowing stench of the unfulfilled
through the deafening noise of a thunderous night…

As I wait for the dawn to shine
with my restless hope for what it might bring
perhaps less lines drawn in the sand
perhaps just one more song to sing?

Avin

Daydreams can take me wherever I want
creating a bridge between fake and real
trotting down that pathway, I feel elated
living in a bubble of dreams, so surreal
besides knowing the norms of reality
acting like a child elevates my spirit
believing in my dreams, I move on in life
harbouring positivity,
striving in the best way fit
sadly when I hit a wall
of failure, of despair, of error
I gather the stardust of my lost wishes
to trail my way of dreaming again, forever

Meenakshi Malhotra

INK HEARTS AND WISHFUL THINKING

I sympathise with the writers for this curse,
conceiving descriptions in crippling agony,
in mending –
evoking our emotions.

How fearsome we move with the timeline,
shackled by words that never break off,
by the inability to avoid definition
and heavy observations –
as we attempt to ground ourselves
in the present.

TO BE CONNECTED TO OUR FEELINGS –
so too our dreams.

Wishful thinking.

How frightening the world appears to be
through the uncharted crevice of memory,
as we release the weight of our heads
from ink-stained palms.

I understand –

In the way time itself could never stop
and discern the fixation,

in the way of a single person who is capable of uplifting
the weight of our burdens,

in the way our only saviour is the one who holds the pen,

the one who fights to survive the breaks in time,

the one that swears there is a legitimate reason to build a time
machine -
not to go back but to simply skip ahead to the good parts,

the one who dares to breathe words like hope and dream,

the one that endlessly devotes themselves to the outer bounds
region of the mind (where dreams go to perish)

the one who no matter how hard the journey
progressed to be,
insists and draws upon the only strength
that remains in a past persona
and declares
"this is why we revisit them everyday,
why we find a pen and paper
and tell ourselves –
'I can make them stay' ".

Shaye Wallace

Answers To My Wild Fantasies

Once I crossed over my wild fantasies and wondered...
"What would be the course of events if
the existence of living eliminates,
the waves of oceans all erect,
the reserves of sunshine go empty,
the flora and fauna all eject?

the passion for art elopes,
the greed for motivation expires,
the value of virtues excretes,
the urge for happiness extorts?

the source of love extinct,
the origin of thoughts erodes,
the urge to pray expels,
the feeling of compassion explodes?"

To which I replied...
"the hymn of death will echo,
the acts of demons will flourish,
the man slaughter will prevail,
the blood bath will only nourish...

the world will only be in chaos,
the imagination will run wild,
they'll all fall prey to lust,
indiscrimination will only rise..."

As I wondered in amazement, my inner voice
raised..."RIGHTLY SAID..."

"The painful hardships will only elevate,

The dreadful era will only come to an end,
The curse of hell will only evaporate...
Only when GOD'S GRACE will be emitted,
Sufferings will be erased, only when Spirituality will be
embraced..."

Twinkle Jain

<u>midnight</u>

what is a dream
but the soft mouth of madness?

here – we are immortal
and she enjoys the slow burn of the reverie

midnight places a well-timed wink upon her gaze
and makes pinky pact promises
that knock on every door
in the hallways of her mind

donned in delicate slumber,
she hangs onto every softly spoken syllable
caching moments that arouse her senses

what they do not tell you is
in a true love story, nothing is absolutely true
just like that of a dream

reality blurs and burns
she inhales the vapors of the other world
and she shakes free

just over the horizon
a pendulum oscillates
–an uneven scale
from delight
to delirium

Kelsey Singh

'Heat-hazed love, now forgone.'

Watching you from afar
Was my summer suicide.
I've been craving your
Lingering taste of summer
Since a lifetime ago.

Standing beneath
Cerulean skies,
You've stained
The color of my skin.
This golden facade
Veiled with honey
Stole my shade of ivory.
My dear summer saudade
Cursed me eternally in
The shape of sunlight.

Goodbye, goodbye.
I'm lost, left
Alone to die.
You vanished
Despite my implore.
Your warmth forever
Stained cold then
Washed ashore.

You are the whole of my heart–
Who burns holes in my heart.

Karen Chan

172

Roses on Fire

Sitting on top of my dresser,
A vase of roses, red and white.
The black rose adorns it midway,
A burning candle jar next to it.
Disguised as the good,
All the promises I'll break,
All the secrets buried in the deep,
That I'm too attached to throw away.
And they still thrive, the reds and whites.
As the sunsets arrive, so does darkness.
A sea of light, happiness befalls too.
The glass jar shatters, the candle still burns.
Petals of red and white, now charred and alit,
The vase now abandoned and blazing.
The deep red trickling through my hands
holding onto the last flower tight.
Yesteryear memories left, tomorrow embraced,
The black rose, my paradise.

Nikitha Senny

The Unimagined

They say Capricorns are so down to earth,
but they forget that we were created in the stars.
I've been digging my heels into the dirt for so long
that I had to relearn how good a fantasy feels,
unrestrained and running through my mind,
its hooves in my chest, gently quaking my lungs,
and I am ecstatically kicked up in confetti
of broken-openness back to the unimagined.

Katherine Cota MacDonald

<u>Dawning</u>

Our days are but dreams
our hopes, shadows
waiting for light.

Our stars still shine on
unseen, wishes caught
beyond the night.

Amanda Waldron

Lost Wishes

Adrift

I should have known
not to make a home
inside your heart
when my own
was feeling
lonely
now when we part
I find myself floating
lost, longing for the
safety I felt in the
weight of your
embrace

Laura Lewis

The Weaver of Woes

Amidst indigo shadows

and arcane mists,

down the pewter pathways

of an ancient forest,

she sits sheltered amongst

tangled oak trees

and weaves whispers

of sorrow, into wreaths;

lacing together memories

and moonlit scars

with unfulfilled wishes

and fallen stars.

Jennifer Torvalson

If Only Then

If only I never tickled the ivories at age seven,
If only I never picked up an axe at age ten,
If only I never gigged in rock bands at age eleven,
If only *then*, I *stopped* my stairway to heaven.

If only I never went to a music high school,
If only I just played what I thought was cool,
Instead of spending hours on the classical,
practicing, perfecting the proper technical.

If only I never played in many projects at once,
If only I just stuck to playing punk rock,
If only my axe teaching business had flopped,
If only *then*, I sang my swan song,
before my *whole life* stopped.

Maybe then, I'd have a normal life
with normal health, be a normal housewife.
Instead, my body broke down.
I'm bedbound, *reeling* in resentment
with no *return*-on-investment.

Chrissie Hyde

The weight in my chest is sudden,
pulling me down
as decades of dreams fall.
The room expands,
an echo of the gulf between us,
my gasping breath sharp in the silence left by the slammed door.
The world becomes a blur
as I hold my breath,
the tears mutiny and fall.
I am lost,
unravelling pieces of identity
alongside the plans we created together.
I press my back to the wall, seeking the support
you have pulled away,
my legs shake as I fall.
The ground meets me,
its touch the opposite of the quicksand I expect
as hope walks away.

Adeola Sheehy

<u>Broken</u>

through broken TV screens, I sit watching everyone go about
their lives,
celebrating, living, loving,
like a movie I have seen before many times, yet I have now
gained a new perspective of
those who have not had their heart shattered like shards of
broken glass, constantly cutting through skin,
opening wounds, like white-hot pokers to the heart, so deep,
you will do anything to escape the grasp of the pain holding
you hostage
if you have not walked through the valley of the shadow of your
own metaphorical death,
you do not know this pain I speak of,
you do not know my pain,
you do not know me

labels create shame and pave ways to excuses for those who we
needed
empty sentiments like loaded guns wound deep, fatalities to the
spirit
you pick yourself knowing you would never be able to survive
another loss like this,
but you go ahead and risk it all anyway

society is not kind to women
who need to feed their souls,
we are told we must let go, but not too much, move on, but not
too quickly
there is no uniqueness to our plight
as the world would rather have us doused in blackness and
consumed by the flames of those who "love" us.

I wake up from nightmares in which he survives
and must explain we can no longer be,
this is my life now

Daydreams & Lost Wishes

as the pain in his face rips my heart from my being,
these are the haunting themes that I get to see,
even behind closed eyes there is no release,
I'll trade them with you, you can have them for free

there is no cure to this "disease" you call grief,
not this one at least, but you prescribe them with ease
side effects of this malignancy to which you cannot reprieve

spare me your niceties please,
you're offensive at best,
not all of us can subscribe to these fairytale themes

I would go anyplace to get some relief,
MAKE. IT. STOP. PLEASE.
but it doesn't care, as you beg and plead on your knees
at this cemetery on the hillside.
I bury fragments of myself into the ground,
resigned to visiting my own grave before it is my time to reside
there.
I do not belong anywhere, anymore,
but on this dew-laden grass, I feel appreciated as
we both silently stream our tears for the departed,
reflections of light shown down upon the once open ground
where we laid you to rest,
but rest is not what follows in the aftermath,
there is no solace for the most damaged of souls,
half-human, half-ghost,
merely shadows of moments from a past life
I miss most.

Amy Laessle-Morgan

Mr Wrong

Please forgive me,
I thought you were he,
But I realize now I was wrong.
I believed you were the beat of my heart—
To love and to cherish until death did us part.
How did I lie to myself for so long?

I see now that you aren't my truest love,
The safe and strong arms that I can be sure of,
The home where I would forever stay.
But the illusion is shattered,
Time wasted, heart battered,
Which is why I must now walk away.

It was my partner I sought in your eyes—
Hoped it was you, but realized
I was mistaken to let myself fall.
Not the love of my life,
And it cuts like a knife,
Because you aren't that man after all.

Mistaken identity, tragic but true,
For I had truly hoped he might have been you—
The soulmate to whom I belong.
And so now I see
That you could never be he,
For I recognize you now, Mr. Wrong.

Raya Soleil

185

Culminated Ruination

I felt the pain starting,
As bones broke through flesh.
They were small at first,
Letting my body slowly adjust.
I welcomed the aching, stretching,
Knowing it was the culmination
Of my dreams.

Soon enough they were ready.
Thin bones with talons at the end,
Membrane stretched between.
They were beautiful.
I wrapped them around myself
Then stretched them wide,
Prepared for flight.

I knew that I was different now,
Unique from all the rest.
I dreamt these into existence,
Becoming all I wanted.
The others didn't see the beauty,
I was strange and odd and cursed.
I reacted too late.

I felt the pain starting,
Different from before
As they pulled and cut,
Tore away what I made.
Laughing at my tears.
Now there's nothing but scars and memories
And dreams of what it was to fly.

K.R. Wieland

A Pit Of Darkness

tonight, the stars come as answers
to your supplication but what can a

tiny fissure in the sky do to a boy dredged in a pit of darkness.

what you really desire is the sky
to fall like a glass ceiling into a million shards

& unveil the razing bioluminescence of your god
till darkness is burnt into a smoky ascent

& your path out of this canyon of depression is illuminated.

say, his light is your compass
to flee from the abyss of solitude.

but the night is like a blindfold
& here you remain shackled in
the web of your thoughts,

agnostic if there can be any light
after this night.

Adesiyan Oluwapelumi

For You

For you

I miss

Steel-strung

Stars

And ink

Dipped

In silent

Confession.

Bold lips

Pressed

And breath

As warm as

Earth

Tilled loose

In penance.

Soft hymns

Sung

As dusk

Moves to take

The sun.

A faded

Mellow sky

Come

So easily

Undone.

For you

I miss

The ghost of

Brushstrokes.

Fingertip to

Supple skin.

A delicate

Touch

To slowly

Drown

In.

For you

I miss

Everything.

Emily R. Paget

Exile

Magnificent Nature has
its own way of creating
harmony where there is
discord, of bringing balance
where it is found wanting.
No wonder the two of us met.
I, with a heart full of love
to pour, you whose
tombstone of a heart
was cold and lifeless
at its very core.
Our love, now,
plays truant,
it lives in exile,
hungry and parched
with a tired, frail voice,
it has forgotten its
former luminous vein.
This is what it is now,
and thus, it shall remain.

Priti Tiwari

Unfinished

My swan song remains unsung.
Been seven suns since my last live strum,
my head first spun, my nervous breakdown begun.
My blood-sugar-magic musical life, suddenly done.

My sole goal ever since I was seven:
be the guitarist playing the next *Stairway To Heaven*.
Cut teeth over two decades of music training.
One-track-mind, no room for failing.

Whether rock, pop, punk, funk, classical or acoustic,
I gigged, taught, absorbed it all, a connoisseur of music.
Many stages opened, the baddest one and my blazed body blew
it.
Standing on shaky ground, I lost my footing, my fast-free life as
I knew it.
It doesn't matter how well one plays, without the wellness to do
it.

Spun out from seeing stars, chronically dizzy and fatigued,
I've chased down every remedy, but can't get no satisfying
relief.
Nobody but me can perceive my persisting unnerving
sensations
that taunt me daily in transient waves, with brief moments of
cessation.

So I drew a line in the sand, tried to bury the past behind me.
Got well enough to go back to university, got the Plan B
marketing degree.
Went from playing three-hour gigs to three-minute songs as a
YouTube hobby.

After graduation, my glass heart cracks led towards relapse.
Spring came in with the breeze, brought fresh-cut hayfever
allergies
re-shattering me with severe vertigo and GAD PTSD.
Another nervous breakdown, back to being mostly bedbound.
Head pounding, sounding *Wake Me Up When September Ends.*

My second time in Wonderland, Almost Alice forgot I
recovered before.
Armed with a therapy plan, at first, could barely stand five
minutes out the door.
I couldn't feel my legs or feet, scared to collapse walking down
the street.
Every few minutes, resting on benches, a thirty-year-old retiree.
Dizzy, detached and numb, as if someone beside me held a gun.
Two to three months in, could walk through shopping malls
again.
Seven months, strolling all terrain, slowly feeling more humane.

No matter the months or years, driving back and forth recovery
road,
rock n' roll fantasies always helped me cope with life's hard
realities.

So still, I hold on to the hope that this will all make sense someday.

If ever I'm past this health fight, if the tides of time give enough respite,

I'll be taking to the stage, channelling Jimmy Page for a second summer take.

Chrissie Hyde

I remember the air,
The sway of the moon.
How the dark lengthened into dawn
& flashes of sweet anticipation
devoured the sun.
I sit here and think harder,
remembering the way you tasted
& how you summoned goosebumps on
my skin, soaking my dreams in rain.
This is how I always want to remember
you...totally unspoiled,
Like the tail of a kite blowing freely
in the wind,
Lingering in my primitive lungs,
Sailing the oceans of my lonesome heart.

[You Are Forever With Me]

Clare McKeown

I wanted to text you

I wanted to text you,   but I didn't.

I almost called you,   but I couldn't.

I was dying to hug you,   but thought I shouldn't.

I even imagined kissing you,   knowing I wouldn't.

I wanted and wanted, yet I stood my ground. A conflict
induced by an old inner wound.

But then, in the still of night,

you texted me.
You called me.

You hugged me,

you even kissed me.

You opened that wound with me, knowing I was afraid. You
let me see your wound too, together we were brave.

But then, in the morning light,

I woke up.

Choked up,

remembering we broke up.

Emma Hill

My everything

Maybe that is what it would take,
An accidental dial of your number,
To make me realise that in the end,
I was just an option,
Not worth the effort.
The truth was needed.
But damn, does it still make it hard to breathe.
It hurts because in that very moment,
I realise you were never just a horizontal dance to me.
You were and are
My Everything.

Nicole Carlyon

I remember when I was young and naive,
I used to have such big dreams squeezed in the tiniest of rooms.
They were bigger than me and you,
Blissfully unaware of how life could get so blue.
That one day my breaths would need to be timed from one to two,
That one day I won't be a child anymore yet society would dictate everything I do.
That one day the fairy-tale of my daydreams would end, run over by demons, monsters and their unruly crew.
Now every time I close my eyes I don't see my father's smile that made everything alright,
But his casket being lowered in the ground and my mother's heart wrenching howls.
The kitchen no longer smells like my grandmother's famous chicken pot pie,
But like microwaved pizza that I ordered last night.
The warmth of my family's embrace now feels like a lie,
As when the sun goes down the cold wafting off their ghosts chills me to my spine.
Even my imagination can't twist up a story I could escape in and feel fine,
Is not being a child anymore really that much of a crime?
The days I can get myself out of bed are long and in between,
But the days my feet touch solid ground I tell myself I still have dreams.
They aren't grand or royal enough to impress some dream jury,
They are smaller and simpler just like I want my life to be.
This emptiness and this dark abyss have swallowed everything glittery and shiny my child self dreamed once upon a fantasy,
Leaving nothing but a deep longing to be happy with

everything I have grown to be.

A dream small enough to finally fit in a room but not my life apparently.

Amal Adnan

The Dreamer's Fight

My thoughts are a battlefield:
fears scattered everywhere like landmines,
memories exploding, shrapnel flying,
questions tearing through the air, unrelenting as rifle-fire,
hopes hiding in the haze and gun smoke
of the grand delusions I call my dreams.
And my mind lays there,
on the scarred, scorched earth,
in tatters.

Julia Yee

collapsed wishes

thoughts get carried away,
leaves me longing each and every day,
for times that were and those to come;
lost in thought, i do succumb.
to cast a spell to materialize,
unfold dreams before my eyes.
reality steals those dreams from me.
she leaves behind sorrow for all to see.
dreams became far and few,
my sight then filled with darkened hues.
so fleeting moments fell out of grasp,
and lost wishes they did all collapse.

Amanda Thuy

Tearstained

salt water
dries on my
cheeks, shining
like glass when
the light passes
through.

will these days
leave a lasting
mark on me?

Laura Lewis

Blue

I loved his big teddy bear eyes. I got lost in the mocha playgrounds they immortalized. Born a Gemini, reaching to symbolize, knowing identical twins pass down generational ties, I would often fantasize that I might be happily surprised. What better way to impress a father who left in distress? How many years did I obsess? I wanted nothing less, than to possess my own beautiful twins to kiss and dress. Oh, and when that day came, I thought I would go insane! I didn't hesitate to proclaim, announce their names, and display their ultrasounds in picture frames.

Oh, but on that fateful day, God took them away. Two became one, as one faded away. Though my dreams were washed in the gray of dismay, to this very day, I can see my lost babe. He picks his favorite color blue, and she lets him, too. Though she'll often lighten the hue. I know he lives in her core every time she picks a new dinosaur, just to keep safe inside her little blue drawer, and I still get to love them both, forevermore.

K. G. Carroll

My dreams are majestic and grand when I'm alone,

like a great white shark, an astounding hunter

with massive jaws and sharp teeth, arrayed with wonder.

But in a room full of people, I feel small

and my dreams shrivel and fall,

like when you realize there's a vast ocean.

Suddenly, there are people with dreams,

like a killer whale far superior to you.

An apex predator with better speed and tactics

or a blue whale far bigger than you,

a creature so gigantic.

How could I not panic?

Tell me, how do I keep my dreams tall

when I feel so small?

Arya Spring

"Lost Wishes"

Sometimes I sit.

I contemplate.

All those years gone by.

How would things have turned out?

I wished things had been different.

I wish I had listened to that voice.

What if.

Reminisce,

What if...

What if that little girl in the shed listened to the whisper in her head? Paid attention to the fear stuck in her throat. What if she listened to her gut, twisted in knots, telling her this was not ok? What if she stood up to him? What if she listened to that voice that told her to be brave? What if she screamed? What if she ran out of the shed, and told on him?

What if that little girl listened to that voice, the one that told her she was worth her teacher's time to listen? What if the teacher had believed that she was telling the truth? What if she stood her ground, and did not give up? What if she told the world what happened? What if she saw the bullies pay for what they had done? What if she spoke, instead of stifling her voice? What if she did not care if she made "trouble" for the wrong doers? What if someone had made her feel worthy of being listened to?

What if that teenage girl listened to that voice? The one that screamed "this isn't ok"? The one that whispered, tell someone, tell someone now! What if she had believed what that voice said? What if the voice was convincing enough to make her believe she was worth more? What if she yelled, "Don't treat me like that"? What if she said, "I don't care who you are!"

What if the college student had paid attention to those warning signs? Taken heed of the messages, would she have found herself there? What if his voice didn't drown out her voice? What if her voice was loud enough? What if she had tuned in and ran out?

What if the young woman had listened? What if she listened to the voice that told her she was enough? What if she had cleared the clutter in her mind, so she could feel the weight of what was being told to her. What if she were able to quiet the negativity so that she could comprehend the thoughts? What if she accepted the words that were whispered to her back then? What if she had made sense of her chaos earlier? What if her negative talk was replaced with positive? What if she had just let someone read her journal, just once. What if she did not make excuses for him? What if she did not protect him for so long? Where would she be now? Where would they all be now?

What if that little girl had shouted from the rooftops? What if she was courageous like her hero in the fairy tales? What if she told the secret? Where would she be now? How would life have been different…? How would her fairytale have played out; would she have married her prince?

What if that teenage girl had stood her ground? What if she ousted him? What if she didn't melt into the woodwork, but instead used her voice to fight and put words in the air about the atrocities? Would she have become the young woman that stayed in such a horrendous circumstance? Or would she have proceeded with caution and have decided **HE** wasn't worthy of **HER**? Would she have had the confidence to leave earlier?

What if the college student had stayed in that night, listening to her gut telling her to stay put? Would she have become a different woman that made different choices?

What if those red flags in early womanhood sent her into action, not bystander? What if she put her foot down? What if she said she deserved more? Where would she be now?

So many years, I ignored that voice. My best friend, my confidant, my supporter, my biggest cheerleader. She has always been there, by my side, whispering softly. I ignored her; instead, I listened to what others wanted, and denied my desires. I took others' wants and needs as mine, I put myself last. I followed what I SHOULD do.

I quieted her, convinced that I would be loved if I…

What if I had listened?

What if? is a hard memory.

Where would I be? Where would my life have gone? What would I have accomplished?

Who would I be? Who would we be?

Audrey Costa

Yesterday's Hopes

Colors flicker in the midnight sky,
Purple hues, majestic, glorious, profound.
Meanings undiscovered,
Though we wish we knew.

Sounds in the night resonating
From places we visit but truly never know,
Muffled and obscure,
Mystical and melodic.
A glimmer in an unknown world.

Dreams pile up onto yesterday's hopes,
Unfulfilled but restrained,
Looking without ever seeing,
Feeling without ever being,
Hoping without ever knowing.
A shadow of an unseen world.

Again, the colors flicker in the midnight sky.
Their brilliance is gone,
Becoming obscured,
Fading into darkness
Until all that remains is what once was.

Or maybe…
Simply nothing at all.

Tammy Muehlfelder

<u>SEASONS OF CHANGE</u>

Our fervour was apricity's embrace
As neon streaks awash a Nordic night.
It flared unfettered through the carapace
Of clotted clouds to cast its fluid light.

Accrescent cravings bloomed in brumal air.
We whispered vows in springtime's silver moon.
As fireflies, we sparked a summer flare,
But in autumnal gilt we were bestrewn.

Alas, the winds destroyed our nurtured nest
And branches wept in tears of brittle leaves.
Our honeyed hive engulfed in flames to breast,
Succumbed to fate and now the woodland grieves.

And thus, a season's smouldering memoirs
Were laid to rest bedecked with vintage scars.

Stuti Sinha

Imaginary hopeless daydreams

wandering in the evergreen land
I stand
daydreaming...
the child in me,
awaiting...
an innocent
blossoming rose
with petals to warm my skin.

there! comes a beautiful flower
she is all too sweet
whilst, emotions sour

desperate for a seed
to breed offsprings

eyes meet,

entangled for a together, forever
melody of a heartbeat.

you and I,

like a bird feather,
our love soars
haphazardly
yet, landing
back on my feet.

as this,
wool gathering fleeting moment
comes to an end.
I hear a voice calling out,
Carmello
my mind takes on the present seat, my friend

this poem " imaginary hopeless daydreams"concludes it's
lines too
with a bitter sweet feel
and a longing for hope
that one day
those dreams will become real.

Carmello Fabri

<u>The Bookmark</u>

I see you in the fading mist:

A lingering shadow;

In my mind adrift

I wonder oft,

Where you tread and trail,

How blessed the earth,

Where your feet prevail.

Under which skies

Do you breathe and sigh?

Amidst which trees

Do you dream and lie?

Which hills embrace you

In their arms

When the gentle winds,

Whisper you Psalms;

Distant you are,

Like a far-fetched dream,

My arms outstretched,

But unreaching you seem.

Oh! lend me a piece

Daydreams & Lost Wishes

Of your sky

And take a teardrop,

From my eye,

And like a bookmark, keep

In a book,

That rests somewhere

In your favourite nook.

And someday perhaps,

When you sit down to read,

Those pages and flip,

Your fingers may lead,

To the page bookmarked,

In a forlorn year,

And you'd hold in your hand

My lonely tear.

RS

<u>The List</u>

I love the way
you wear your joy
like a candy necklace
you're looking to share.
I love the passion
in your voice
when you speak of things
that matter,
and also things that don't.
Your mind is a library,
an eclectic collection
I'd love to sift through
and study.
I love the way
your fingers bounce
with unused energy,
making me want to hold them
in mine.
I love how you smile
like you have a secret,
and I long to know what it is.
I could list all the reasons
I could love you,
but there's one reason
I can't,
and it outweighs
everything else.

Cate McMinn

LOST WISHES ON FALLEN STARS

It is all in my head,
Daydreams and lost wishes
Of our haunted love story.
Lifetimes filled all existing notebooks,
We are trying to write on
An already written page.
Wor(L)ds overlap and bleed
Into each other,
Reality and imagination flirts
With our left over (in)sanity.

We sit there in a forgotten field,
Watching time disorient between us,
Hoping for a version of us
That will last together in this lifetime.
We daydream,
We make wishes
Upon fallen stars of our starless sky.

They all fell, dead, buried below earth.
We keep burying our souls there,
Playing pretend to live.
Lost wishes on fallen stars.

Cathy Blue

The Agony of Defeat

I found her,
perched and ready for flight,
her wings finally strong enough,
her bloat cautiously confident enough,
to carry her to that nearby platform in the sky –
that one that's seemed so close, yet so far.

She knew this was her chance to shine,
a long-shot though it was.
After all, there'd be others to help with the journey from that
stage,
and surely her eagerness and enthusiasm,
her vulnerability and heart,
her passion and persistence,
all marked her as ready, she reasoned, even if the semantics
weren't yet as polished as she imagined they probably wanted.

But in the eleventh hour
her perch was crushed under the weight of timing's choice,
the blow of not-yet-meant-to-be
harder to withstand than she anticipated,
and she crumbled in defeat.

She wants to believe her journey isn't over,
only temporarily stalled in neutral until
that first gear called Will, is reengaged,
but for now she cries out in despair
because the wind has been taken from her sail,
again,
and she is left to find both new courage,
and a new platform.

When will the chance to fly come again,
she wonders?
Will it ever?
Oh, to soar the world on the wings of words
and slay the darkness with the promise of hope.
Is this asking too much?

For now, she returns to the still waters
where she dreams of giving more,
and where her heart says there is no time to wallow.
For she can hear the world whisper,
"Come, do not tarry in the fields of rejection,
or become tangled in the brambles of self-doubt,
for you are needed…
there is much work to be done."

Christine Colyer

<u>Hidden</u>

Once a light so full of light,
I now cling for recognition in the darkness.
A faded crescent, a sliver of the light I once was.
I wait for a strong enough telescope to find me.

Once a flower so bright,
I now hide among pages,
a pressed version of the beauty I once was.
I wait to be discovered among the pages I hide between.

And now, I dream of the day
I will have the vision to see.
I dream of the day
I will have the strength to unfold.
I dream of the day
I will no longer be dreaming.

Debie Collins

<u>Procrastination</u>

Drive myself crazy,
pacing, thinking
of all that was, is and could be.
Living in a world of dreams,
the days pass me by,
grasping at lost moments,
past opportunities,
desperation
makes it hard to breathe –
is there still a chance to be
what I might have been?
Still I live in hope,
no time for despair –
but why is it so hard to just
get
things
done?

Angela Olejnik

Pieces of Me

As I look down
all that I see
are tiny scraps of
littered debris.

They are pieces of me…
fragments of a life,
shattered and scattered,
lost hopes and dreams.

I grasp at the pieces,
desperately,
as they blow away
into the sea.

I watch them float on,
sorrowfully.
As the waves wash away
all that's left of me…

Shelley Sanders-Gregg

There was a time she loved so much, she thought her heart
would burst.
Can you remember the rush of feeling so free, giving like that?
It's a mix of all the things you thought could be your favorites.
Until it's not.
Then the memories leave salty tears when she sees them
Instead of the warm hum they once elicited.
She thought at first he might have grown tired and just needed
a break.
But what she couldn't know was that what was inside him never
rested.
It just lurked there under the surface long enough to make her
feel wanted.
Sometimes in dreams he was still all she ever needed. Until she
awoke.
And another day of making herself small, not to draw his
attention.
As the chamber around her heart grows thicker, she wonders if
she will dare
To give her heart so freely ever again.

Dawn P. Harrell

Distant dreams

Countless sighs, countless smiles, countless miles, till I counted; 10,497 miles there are, or there were, are still, between us. Miles of ink spills of trust and love, now gone with the wind. Miles never to be travelled, souls never to meet, walks never to be taken, places we won't sit and eat. Sunsets we wouldn't watch, cocktails we wouldn't drink, play fights never started, no giggles, no winks.

No picnics in the park, observing local art,

No holding hands or having heart-to-hearts.

No movies, no museums, and no plays.

No dancing, so no hips ever swayed.

No bookshops, garden strolls or picking seeds to plant,

no dramatically comparing how brightly you bloom against our roses and the moon.

No reading books with you catching me smile, just a whole bunch of grapes that I won't feed you.

Countless movies you'll never watch with my head resting on your chest, breathing in your heavenly scent, with me contemplating if you were heaven-sent.

The possibility of us not making it; was never sensed.

Every plan we had, was lost, our love never to be found again. Memories linger for every breakfast I never made and lunches you'll never taste; all that remain are moments that our souls were reaching out for one another, such a waste.

Desserts never shared, candles never lit.

No legs wrapped around your waist as I sit.

No days at the beach, or drinks at the bar, no forest adventures,

No deep desire and vulnerabilities shared

equals no surrenders.

No boat rides or late-night drives.

No kissing your neck or stroking my thighs.

No fingers through your stupid hair.

No baths ran, with showers shared.

No glances, no soul-to-soul stares,

No laying under star-filled skies,

No open fires, no playing chess, no sighs.

No evening river walks, or late-night talks,

No midnight massages or morning coffee kisses

No wandering the world together, no satin sheets, cotton t-shirts, with our tattoos kissed as often as lips.

No, me in heels, no, you in ties, because you don't travel to a place where love doesn't reside.

No placing my happiness in your hands, no hoping we will meet one day and remember how in love we used to be.

No standing up for a love who never stood up for me, especially those who never truly understood, for love isn't something you don't understand, under any circumstances beyond how many times I was understanding, giving you second chances.

No growing old together, no keeping each other young, no being ready for the greatest love we found. No, nothing, no more, we are done.

No swoon or I'll see you soon, no meeting you and imagining my wildest dreams came true.

Ally Bird

Daydreams & Lost Wishes

There's a space in the bed
Cold sheets
Unused pillows
A mattress that never moves
Your weight isn't there
No breath but my own

I stretch my limbs
I am not big enough
The space remains
It niggles at me like a forgotten word
It itches like staring eyes on my back
You are not here

Adeola Sheehy

NOSTALGIA

—

Objects are further than they appear this time
As the city fades in the review mirror
Mountains and trees grow along the skyline
Memories of you and I playback in my mind like a cinema
An ache of nostalgia
Fireside wine as smoke billows like clouds in a dream
Music sings softly in the background as my heart tugs at the
strings
and my breath makes waves in the night sky
Summer to an end and an autumn awakening

Jena P. August

Upon a Placid Lake

Upon a placid lake

between two mountains

of lingering heartache

and a vast canyon

of sepia memories...

    I quietly drifted away.

In my ragged vessel

I carried the mourning

of long-forgotten dreams.

For time and aging had

whittled away at the

    essence of who I had been.

I looked at the water below

and saw a reflection,

rippled and shimmery.

The image appeared as

an unfamiliar woman

    staring back at me.

In every wrinkle and

each splintered line

was my life, its entirety.

Like a roadmap of

rugged terrain across

    a weathered tapestry.

And I noticed, from this

perspective, there was

a certain solemn dignity.

As if this life had more

significance than I'd

    ever thought, previously.

Perhaps, the dreams I

thought I'd lost weren't

gone, as it had seemed;

Instead, transformed into

a greater version, as shown

    in the face looking back at me…

Shelley Sanders-Gregg

A Letter to Lost Wishes

To my lost wishes of grey and blue,
We used to be the best of friends, only now you seem like a lost
lover, like a heartless heartbreaker.
You taught me to let go when all I ever wanted was to hold on
to you eternally, tragically, hopelessly.
You made the candle of hope in my heart flicker, flicker, flicker
till it was out, till I was out.
You surely do know how to break a heart so loud, silence
cannot contain the sound that turns ultrasonic.
You got lost only to be found again, and again, and again, in
the deep crevices of my soul like a song on repeat.
Nobody knew my heart as you did and perhaps, nobody ever
will.
For it's so changed that it now seems foreign even to me.
Veins that once pulsated with the warmth of my blood now
seem to want to give in to the cold of my melancholy.
But no, every time I close my eyes, you still cannot change how
I dream on.

– the voice you never heard

Divya Singh

Flotsam

Dreams caught in the riptide
    the strong currents carrying them
        far out of reach
      helpless, I bob and drift
    as I watch them
washed away on wayward waves
    dragged to desolate shores
        frantic, I try to wave down
    a passing boat
but when it reaches me
    I see it is empty…
        rudderless
      oarless…
    just a hull of peeling paint
a mast of crucified hopes.

Amanda Waldron

229

Some Dreams Evolve

while appearing to subsist in normality

encircled by lights of love and security—

not every shape of life we encounter

floats on calm mirrors of untainted waters

unforeseen and sudden—many hopes

drift far beyond the safety of any lifeboat

even our eyes—glazed over in wetness—

from the incessant trials of our family

laden in lonely voids of cancerous maladies

or stormy waves of darkening depression

now peer through dry tears of lost dreams

even our moistened pillows fail as a remedy

when we abruptly awaken upon arid sands

that fold us into their desolate fiery desert

our faltering paths sink into indigo fears

beneath its dark and unforeseen presence

we long for any blessed mercies that appear

common among countless other families

but our veiled cries seem to never surface

so—after a long spell in our pity party—

we came to discover—time after time—

other numerous souls sailing a coarser life

beyond our sharpest years ever imagined

beyond old words that confined us in walls

gradually—deeply—seeds of empathy

took root in the soils of our experiences

and sprouted inside our cultivated spirits

our twisted trees rose under ruddy skies

but bent in the stiff howling winds of life

we blossomed—but in unexpected shapes

now—as we attempt to take it all upon us

surrounded by a heaping talus of troubles

burdened beneath the heavy shadows

of the family that we ceaselessly love—

we try to wear hurts awkwardly inside

while painting it gracefully on the outside

believing life's grinds in scarcities of light

trapped in our own fractured red clay pots

Daydreams & Lost Wishes

of time should rain all their sadness down

upon our stronger and better patient hands—

to lift our younger, pure, and innocent heads

upon stronger wings of our flowing hope

that in all our rawest of errant disorders—

our imaginary boundaries of us and them

we might slowly but softly learn to adapt

to reach beyond our confusion of pains

and fix up whatever stuff may remain

within our worn-out tears of emptiness

for in our languishing corridors of society

we learned to brush on eyes of light—so that

when anyone questions—"are we okay?"

we simply say "yes"—to offer a kind face

yet deep inside our hearts—we know

our hurts curl up in these short fake smiles

we learned to live in slices of our dreams

in moments of younger—more eager eyes

using their sweetest words as our songs

we pray for their courage to find real peace

and in all our visions inside sounder hopes

we dream of reinforcing their lofty dreams

our pains discovered greener joys as we

mined out short momentums of service—

we conjured in other's shadows of doubt

to depend more on a combined strength

with those who walk upon far steeper paths

as one—we labored on—to return their light

and in our unique but grief-stricken ways

on wild rivers or plains—unanticipated

we ultimately discovered that in the end—

we all float together and are healed

together in a colorful quilt of unity

one—we are still learning how to sew

in all our vast prayers of nightly dreams—

protected by enduring remnants of faith

we still reach out to powers far beyond us

and attempt to find a purpose and grace

in the loss of another precious dream

and somehow—we resolve to dream again

but when we are all alone—inside walls

of a darkness—we reserve for ourselves

we snuggle up close—embracing eternity

and we weep under clouds of lost dreams

watering our futures with the loving tears

that evolve a cloud into a greener vision

for a sunnier day and a far brighter hope

Doug W. Evans

You left

You stood above me,

With your shadow casting itself

Right in front of my path,

Shielding me from the excess hope,

Giving me a place

To simply

Exist.

Somehow, your actuality

Was more than enough

To comfort me,

To tell me,

That I'm so close,

So for every second

Of every day,

I would look up

To see you,

Hoping you were inching closer,

Hoping that one of these days,

I would be able to stretch my hand out

And grasp your touch,

To thank you,

To keep you in the midst of my palms

So you could be here

Whenever I needed.

So why aren't you here yet?

Why have you just moved further away?

I don't understand,

I gave you

Everything

That I possibly could.

I put in all that I had in me;

Was that not enough?

Was I not enough?

Siya Sawhney

<u>What Comes After</u>

There's not always something that signifies 'The End.'
No neon lights or street signs. One day you just wake up, and
there it is.
The end to all you've worked for.
And you're left there, wondering,
"What the hell do I do now?"

K.R. Wieland

Death waits for no one –
It has its own rhythms
It speaks its own language
It reveals itself in gradient
textures
It is a place of unbearable
blacks and greys
Where ashes turn to ashes
& dust turns to dust

[Nothing Lasts Forever]

Clare McKeown

A Dream

I stand

At the water's

Edge

Hand outstretched

And face

Caressed

By salt

And the

Evening sun.

The ocean

Swallows me

Whole.

Brushed in painted

Ribbons

Of slate, indigo

And gold.

Silent lessons

In reclaiming

The forbidden

239

Parts of my

Soul.

I cast

A final wish

Into seas that

Taste of

Heartbreak.

The whisper of

Dreams

And a vast ocean

Collide.

Stolen hope

Pulled slowly

With the

Going out

Of the

Tide.

Emily R. Paget

Beautiful distraction:

A chance encounter. An unexpected greet.
A frustrating childish persona at first but kind eyes I came to meet.

His face was young but his soul was old,

It wasn't long before desire took hold.

An unspoken knowing, when near or not around.
Holding back but wanting, we both stood our ground.

So many reasons not to, I did anyway.

I ignored my gut and let my wounded heart lead the way.

It was beautiful, it was brief, it was ours, it was real.

But deep down, I knew I had old wounds to heal.

We said goodbye, as I begged my eyes not to cry.
Neither wanting to let go and both knowing why.

Reality is harsh. But acceptance sets you free.
Accepting he wasn't mine to keep, I refocused on me.

Emma Hill

My Most Beautiful Grief.

Standing on the harrowing reality, my body feels weak.

I'm torn between the urge to either throw myself at him

Or shackle my heart in chains and just sigh deep.

I'm smitten with darkness and his fading silhouette.

And just yesterday, all I could hear was our laughter echoing,

But today its sorrow lying beside me on my bed.

And I just realized that if I ever fall, I won't end up

Laughing as I did with him. I'll sob loudly now.

It's sad that 'We' turned into 'You and I' and then

Strangers walking on a different path altogether.

I read that there are five stages of grief but

What if I get stuck on denial forever and never reach

To the last stage acceptance? What if I'm delusional

And my heart never opens up to someone else?

I wonder if anyone would be willing to give me

A kiss of mercy on my forehead and

Pull me out of the sea of tears after him.

They told me that, " Life won't stop without him."

But what about me? 'Cause I stopped at every step in life

And looked back again to see if there is just a shadow,

Just a sound of his breath, just a thump of his heart behind me.

And no matter how much time passes by,

I know my heart would still hold onto the

Silly things he did, and I'll smile unconsciously.

When I'll look out of the window, my eyes

Would wish to see him at the end of the lane.

Maybe one evening when I'll be stuck in traffic,

I'll decide to make a turn towards him, but I hope I don't.

And now, I've categorized pain in two types;

One: When there are tears in your eyes and

Your whole body aches as if it's shackled.

Second: When there are tears in your eyes yet

A radiant smile on your face, hiding the anguish.

And I think the latter one reminds me that he,

He is my most beautiful grief in life.

Hamna Adeel

What Smiles Can't Hide

Winter has come too soon again. It licks its cold, looking for
warmth between my layers. There's a Cafe closing early in five
so I tip with an extra smile. The toast is burnt. The coffee is
bitter. A reflection of societies current position. Tired from lack
of rhythm. Lost wishes. Worn out and in, made by dreams
postponed. We've aged more than we've lived outside these last
years, and how it shows. Bones turned to stone. Reflecting in
our shells till we broke. Freezing juxtaposed. Slow motion on
fast forward. Living life like this Cafe, a little more openly
closed. A little more dead inside. Full cups of empty. Drinking
what smiles can't hide.

hergreyside

your name sounds like a rhythm of a song

      that i can't stop humming

      it was the beacon in the darkest pit

      it was the greatest poem i ever worshipped

                  until you were gone for good

                    only then i realised

your name was the rhythm of my heartbeat

the reason of me breathing

the moment it was taken from me

the world stopped spinning

and the rhythm that was once a lullaby

will forever haunt me in my sleep

while you live as if there were never us

never me

never a thing

Isabella Quek

Like the Wind

Proving your love

is like trying to

collect the wind.

It's blatantly blustery,

Clearly a cacophony.

So, I rush out

to catch it

in a jar.

Screw the lid on tight

and show it off

to all my friends.

Puzzled,

they cock their heads

and say to me

"But there's nothing there".

Another windy day,

The whispering willow

wails and whimpers.

The gales gleefully giggle.

I frantically photograph

the swaying of the sails.

Document the teetering

of the trees.

But when I look back,

attempt to show off

all the ways your love

shows up.

Everything is still.

No one can see

what was so powerfully,

prominently, present.

And I think the saddest part –

the loneliest realization

is that your love,

for me,

is invisible,

even to you.

Meg Judge

Nightmares

I used to close my eyes
    When I dreamed.
In that place, everything was right,
    Perfect, and beautiful.
After waking, I would see
    That it was true,
Flowers bloomed and birds sang,
    And there was you.
Then reality became dark.
    My world turned gray.
Your words cut deeper than any knife,
    And the flowers wilted.
I try not to dream anymore.
    What point is there?
When I know I will only
    Have nightmares.

K.R. Wieland

the origin of an earthquake

pressure spheres

unidentifiable

wishes in jars

lives lived in flashes of memory

some have turned to stone

(invisible stones cause

even larger seismic waves)

we didn't know how to identify the timing

of things

causes were effects

effects, causes

blind people could not imagine that

they would also cause earthquakes

we were deluded by the non-explanation of science

which could not predict them, exactly

but we have been anchored

in knowing that we could

find explanations

without us committing to anything

(everything we wanted)

but the earthquake came

and we were amazed

with its unconscious layers

and flashes pointing (so accurately!) towards

our fissures

seeing our houses in ruins

walking over objects.

no one could even remember

the useless predictions of consolation anymore

there, we had rubbles

(from the "I"?)

a piece of wood

was no longer a bed

an unrecognizable cup

was no longer a receptacle

a picture frame

did not remind me of your face anymore

a sock without an owner

lived on other places

beyond the closet

what was left of desire

after an earthquake

was the earthquake itself

as potential

bordering everything we were

(before I moved

to San Francisco

I was nostalgic for earthquakes

to imagine what lives

amidst the constant threat of

instability

a reminder of the

imminence of change

to walk over the cracks

on the campus of UC Berkeley

seeing the cracks through the walls of the building

Dwinelle Hall

it was no longer nostalgia

-the imminence of danger

animated everything I was

ancestral traumas)

earthquake presence

earthquake stories

the big one

hovered under a

non-chronological time

(how to encompass

planet earth

in individual times?)

Persephone's study notes:

an earthquake: slide down a toboggan

to Hades

a woman's womb:

to search for volcanic origin

stop before the ecstasy

hold your breath

notice if the uterus contracts

against my commandments

observe

if in contraction

we accumulate

enough strength

for an earthquake

Isadora Grevan

Love at souls sight

For that short space in time, you were my best friend, my soulmate, my one true love.
It was love at soul's sight; even after you were gone, I still genuinely believed that. Until the day that light was shed, and the pain of us not even being real to you hurt me even more than you leaving. My f**king pride made it so much worse, F**K I'm so stubborn just like you told me I was, stubborn just like you, a stubborn pair we were; us two.

In the end, you became the coach whose training consisted of forcing me to kick a ball with a broken foot, and cared not for the agony you caused me in the long run. Whether it was intentional or not matters not. You were the long-forgotten apology that never came, and as much as I despise those lessons that ripped my soul two, GRANTED, you made me stronger and GRANTED you made me wiser, ADMITTEDLY you helped me blossom into who I really am. You cut off my air supply and watched me drown deep within myself, as you misconstrued my all, and abandoned me with no remorse.

You still don't know my side, and now with time, I'm more aware of the extent of yours.

You said you loved me and broke down a lifetime of walls, and I trusted you - shortly after, I watched you go back on every loving word you ever said. And because of us, I now know how to live when one feels like one's heart has died.

Yet sometimes, I push all this pain to one side, and I still find myself saying THANK YOU for those moments in time, as my soul cried and I become more and more aware of myself. As I felt that small part of me that still missed you and wished you were in my life, even as a friend, so that you can see who I've become now. All those threads that went over my head at the time finally made sense. I now have a tapestry in my mind of what I think happened between us, and it kills me when my soul makes eye contact with it.

Exactly two years today, and sometimes I still feel that trauma from my metaphorical broken foot. It still aches under the moonlit skies when I'm reminded of you, of us, and I sigh for the us that I thought we were and the love I thought we both had. My heart just doesn't beat the same since, as every once in a while, it utters your name, your memory from those long lost, forgotten times, still reverberating throughout my soul. I still hear our songs, and in case you didn't know, I was crazy about you.

Sometimes, I defend the thought that I wasn't as meaningless to you back then and that our love was, for that briefest of moments, real. Other times, logic slaps me across the face and shows me my pain, and on occasions, the echoes of truth cause rain to fall down the windows of my soul. I still smile at the thought of our friendship, even though we'll never talk again. Despite everything that I now know, I still don't hate you, I never did, I never could, and I don't think I ever will. I still pray for you, old friend, granted not as often and probably more than you deserve, but my soul never forgot yours; it merely let go.

But the universe sends me reminders sometimes, and honestly, I don't know whether to laugh or f**king cry at the audacity of the stars. It was, after all, two years ago today that I thought my dream came true, the morning you approached me and I spoke to you.

Ally Bird

Purgatory

Sinking into

the subtle sting

of woe,

I kiss goodbye

to yesterday's wishes,

and watch them

silently go,

dissolving into the ether

where my hopes

have no name,

and my dreams

are all dying,

as disappointment

will reign,

for on the cusp

of forever,

my hopes were

cruelly snatched away,

and now I exist

in this purgatory,

immersed in

relentless dismay.

J. Sexton

Maybe Tomorrow

Another morning, she awakes;

a thousand sighs escape.

Curtains drawn, against

the warmth of a welcoming sun.

For its sunlight cannot heal,

or soothe, the damage done.

Another foggy day awaits,

here, in consuming pitch blackness,

she will remain.

Dark delusions; daydreams of

her haunted heart breaking,

repeatedly replayed.

Consuming illusions; memories

distorted, her pain achingly replays.

Maybe, she will rise soon. Maybe.

Days are passing her by unforgivingly;

dawns spawn, afternoons bloom, and

every night a smiling moon swoons.

With each drying tear, she hears

an echo of distant cheers.

Lurking, in the corners of

her mind's shadows, dreams still grow.

The wallflowers of her determined soul.

Soon, their petals will blossom,

outshining the darkness she

has come to know as home.

And, maybe tomorrow, her curtains

will no longer stay closed.

Maria L. Hayward

Kirchhoff, 2020

I conjured up a scenario in my head.

I'd stand and watch something memorable to both of us:

a concert of the band we used to listen to in uni,

the sunrise we both loved chasing, or

the night sky that reminded you of my eyes. You'd approach
me, and without looking I would know it was you, but I would
fight the urge to hold you right then,

a few years since I saw you last,

and I would succeed. You would stand beside me and say, "Did
you miss this?", with your hands in your pockets while I cross
my arms in front of me. There'd be a pause.

I would look at you and after one skip of a heartbeat

look back at the horizon. "I missed you."

I'd reply in that straightforward manner I know you'd have a
bashful reaction to. And you would.

You'd smirk to yourself and start counting the blades of grass on
the ground for one,

two,

three seconds. And I would smile at myself too, with
satisfaction.

I would wish that after a comfortable silence, you'd stand in
front of me,

turn,

and face me. While you search my face for any trace of
hesitation, I'll stare at you with the eyes that you hate (or so you
said,

because to you they seemed to stare fleetingly like a meteor
merely passing by).

Failing at your search, you'd hold me like you've never held me
before.

You never really have.

We'd stay like that long enough to drain me of my pride and
finally,

a lifetime since your last invitation,

I'd respond to your warmth. No words would need to be said.

But that would be wishing for too much.

And that made up scenario will be sealed as is,

in this writing,

for as long as we both refuse each other,

until we are both refused by time.

J. De Ramos

Daydreams & Lost Wishes

they say that the things we lose

find their way back to us at the end

i wasn't sure it is true until

i lost you

it was then that

i started finding you

in everything

everywhere

every orange hoodie is yours

every scent is your perfume

every bright sunrise is

the one we watched together

every heart i look into

has a piece of you

and every time i smile

in front of my mirror i see

that you became a piece of me

Mohammad Allouch

"Grief Has Never Been A River"

Grief has never been a river

It is not in the nature of healing waters

to flow in a single direction

I am lost instead

to the ebb of salted tides

becoming wreckage beneath the waves

Suddenly floating

bobbing peacefully above the surface

A silent observer of the clouds

But the winds of time are known

for their power to churn the stillest waters

My bones are harshly thrown

Surviving on gulps of labored breaths

begging the fickle tides to turn

Drowning once again

Daydreams & Lost Wishes

Grief has never been a river

And so my weary soul will learn

how to live amidst the sea

Swimming near then far

Wondering

if ever my heart will reach the shore

Jennifer Gordon

Wishes Lost to Dreams

I've dreamt of you day and night
In daydreams and in sleep
Your touch as real as breath
I've not felt upon my skin

Wishes for kisses and conversation
Hypnotic stare mistook for love
Butterflies and soul flutters
Bubble gum love in twin flame wrapper

I fell for you by your design
To be your echo and mime
You locked my heart in a cage
I wandered the wilderness of fantasy

My life slipped away
Like sand through your fingers
I was lost between worlds
Caught in a vampires love spell

Julia Sophia Brown

If Only

If only I was an assassin, pirate queen, lady thief, or battle mage:

beautiful, charming, and invincible, with magic that runs through my veins.

If only I was the girl with shining hair and a flashing sword,

who has gleaming eyes, a smart mouth, and a dangerous secret,

who can outrun her enemies and trade stories in multiple tongues,

who is wanted across kingdoms for leading rebellions and fighting against evil kings –

notorious, roguish, fearless, and bold.

If only I was someone else in another world,

maybe then I would stop wishing I was someone else

somewhere other than here.

Julia Yee

<u>Taking Time</u>

"Sorry for taking my time"
I love how she confessed crime,
Mute and blur everybody
To approach me gracefully.

She hasn't aged a decade.
Her elegance didn't fade –
Not her melodious laughter,
Not her eyes' stunning power.

"Sorry for taking my time"
Lingering lines in my mind.
I should have done this sooner –
Experience bliss earlier.

Live my wishes eon-old,
Being drenched, drowned, not by gold.
Rather, by her warmth, her words
Not even gems can afford.

"Sorry for taking my time"

She implied, walking away.

Why did she apologize?

She'll be back soon, right? And stay?

She just got here, now she goes?

Floor floods, roof falls, a wall blows.

Then silence…

Darkness…

A chime.

"Sorry for taking my time".

Delton John M. Go

<u>HUMANS</u>

We try to keep one another, we try to stick

what we know of them to us and wear it

'til it unrolls in the wash,

clean and giddy for new.

To scrape away at paper layers glued

to one another, glued to their first

flat finality,

fingernails pull and preen at edges, color

comes up like an old photo negative, and

we can never fully take what

was never ours.

It will never be the same.

I'll press the too-thin neon tiger eye

between my fingers, its half-ears, some whiskers, no nose,

the other eye so so far away,

its broken stripes echoing

mine not mine.

Katherine Cota MacDonald

The Moon Seems Fuller Tonight

The moon seems fuller tonight;

Shining brighter than the bright,

But the dark is lurking in my mind,

For the milky way is never kind.

From rusty drawers of the heart,

Memories never depart;

Flowing ceaselessly out of crumbling walls,

In mind's old deserted halls;

They waltz and tango amidst my cries,

Subduing my heart's aches and sighs,

The fluttering leaves offer no respite;

Casting shadows on my sprite,

Your tender words fall out of line.

In pirouettes twirl and untwine,

And disappear like the morning mist,

Amidst failing promise of a tryst,

A gloom impending ever so slight,

Like you're there but never quite.

RS

TIME

A song remains unheard
Among the bleak branches that stand frozen.
Every breath is thick as I breathe in fog.
The air is cold and I cannot stop thinking,
Are we meant to face failures?
Or are failures meant to be part of our lives?
Every day, every passing minute,
Are we not just survivors of time?
Are we not struggling to prevent failure,
Or to get through failures?
Isn't everything about or around or for time?

Shanmugaa Bharathi S R

eyes closed

You're the dream I always dreamt

Seeing you for the first time

Knowing you exist in the real world

For a moment, gave me a hope

I could almost touch, you were so close

Looking at you without my eyes closed

Like all dreams though, suddenly I awoke

Before I even had you, I was forced to let go

I think that was just too cruel of life

Dreams are something we hold to cope

Watching them be taken away

Not wondering if it will happen

But knowing that they won't

How do we come back from that?

Watching our fate unfold

Slowly hung by life's rope

Kairos Moira

Abandoned

I promised I wouldn't cry as we said our goodbyes...
The next time you came back, it would be to stay for good.

But as I watched you walk away that cold, rainy day at the
airport... I knew.
Every fiber in my being screamed with the thought...
"If he gets on that plane, he's not coming back."

I pleaded with you to stay.

You got on that plane.

And now all that I have left are a few photographs, a broken
bracelet, two years of memories, a lifetime of future plans made
that will never come to fruition, and your old sweatshirt tucked
safely away at the bottom of my dresser drawer, along with my
heart that beat only for you...

Reminders of what you left behind, of a life that would never
exist.

Valerie Leyden-Morffi

Adieu dear dreams

Visions soaked in lingering scent of my sanity
Daydreams or so you call them, holding up a miserable man like
charity.

The only light in an unnerving eternity of gloom,

It's that fitting puzzle piece, a spell for the fallen souls to bloom.

And so I chase these dreams calling me home

To an abode echoing heartache carols in its magnificent dome.

But as I finally breathe in the air of my supposed freedom,

I break free from the siren song & perceive this mirage, an
illusionary kingdom.

I wonder if it was anything more than a mere castle built in air

Made of knitted words, a gossamer dream that I threaded
without care.

Now what's left, is to kiss all the dreams farewell in a heartbeat

Though I know, mistletoe goodbyes are a bit too bitter for my
taste, a lot less sweet.

Hurts to end this unfinished story by burying the dreams alive

Like the fading glimpses of your favorite memory you're trying
hard to revive.

Now that I've learnt, I'll choose different seeds to reap fruits
riper

And entice the universe to follow me like a *pied piper*.

Shreya S Bharadwaj

"Hopeless Wish"

I cannot give you anything more

Cannot hug or see your face

I miss you for all of my days

Why did you have to leave?

If only you could have stayed

Another year, a week or day

Even that would not be enough

I would keep you forever with me

Many things I never told you

A few things I never showed you

Questions I have no answer to

Many more things we could do

Certain memories etched in me

While others will fade to grey

"Don't worry about me," you said

You must have known your fate

But I will always cherish

The very last thing

You ever spoke:

"Thank you…"

Karuna Mistry

It was the weeping mist and
turquoise tears that helped me
to embrace the insanity of life
Unraveling the truth like
pieces of art
Allowing the rivers beneath
the surface to flow freely
and unrestricted
To give a voice to the words
I could not bear to read out loud...
the unread pages of my heart

[Unread Pages]

Clare McKeown

Permanence

I'm like a meteor,

skimming the Earth's atmosphere,

leaving a trail of debris behind,

floating around in orbit

as a souvenir of my troubles.

I dream of breaking through

the changing air pressure,

passing through the clouds,

touching the ground,

feeling the crunching wood,

and the escaping sea–

On my way down

to the end of my dream,

hoping that this time…

its permanent.

Kathryn Holeton

Move My Scars into View

I wanted to show you, move my scars into view.

Let your fingers read in braille, the holy grail of my skin.

Slip into the epiphany of our soul's eclipse when I kiss your lips.

Your bare hands on my chest, bless my naked heart at rest.

Just once I wanted to pretend, my life wouldn't end,

before drowning in the oblivion of love's epinephrin of sin.

Yet I'm left again in abandon,

to flirt in darkness with ghosts,

avoiding enamored lampposts.

I won't step into the light,

for all I have is the night,

where dreams contrite dance in fantasy's delight.

K. G. Carroll

wonder if

i held on to childish dreams far too long;

through those eyes i righted wrongs.

but life threw lessons my way so grow i did;

thus, i hid away that inner kid.

every so often she tugs at my heart,

but now i've grown far too smart.

calloused skin now covers all,

can't feel a thing when i fall.

yet with each step through life i take,

there is wonder if that child i'll wake.

Amanda Thuy

<u>Prey</u>

trained to be prey
but also not to be too prey
hating oneself for being prey
hiding for being prey
changing to be prey
while inhibiting
the real desire to
be some kind of prey
pretending not to be prey
while being prey
not desiring much
cause then you are
preyed upon
not letting desire
overtake you
cause you are
woman and it could
be dangerous
no right to feel
too much
cause your function
is to be silent
accept your prey
status
never hunter
don't be too sexy
too pretty
too loving
too anything
take care of everyone's
right to live

but your own

let your self
be someone else's
ownership
cause life is too precious
and you must be told
what to do
otherwise you will be prey
but not the prey you need to be
your body
does not belong to you
it's other
don't dare suck
someone else's milk
don't dare crave
and need
since you must be
a receptacle for cravings
and obey

Isadora Grevan

Remembrance Of A Dream

I dreamt a dream yesterday,

What a bittersweet memory,

We were walking side by side,

Lost in each other's warmth you see,

It was a beautiful city,

So alive and free.

I dreamt a dream today,

It was a bittersweet memory,

I was walking alone,

It was cold you see,

What a painfully beautiful city,

Still so alive and free.

For a moment I thought I took the wrong alley,

But how sad, it was never a dream you see.

I was lost and alone in this bittersweet memory.

Now only your footsteps echoed in this beautiful and sad city

My, what a tragic reality has my dream come to be.

Meha Khan

Daydreams and lost wishes

Reveries created in my mind

Infinite world of possibility, being defined

Carried away to the fantasy island

Sandcastles of dreams, being planned

Hopes and wishes comes crashing down

As the violent sea gushes in and I drown

Everything seems like a plight of lie

Aching to be alright

Lakshyaa Velmurugan

SHE WAITS

As she waited to board her plane, she had hoped to see his face.

Maybe it was better like this.

She hated goodbyes anyway.

He did not appear.

They had not even met.

Now so many years later, she still waits,

looking at the phone, willing it to ring.

Outside it starts to rain.

If only it could wash away her pain.

She knows the phone will never ring and doubts whether he
even thinks of her.

But still, she waits for that call.

Maggie Watson

<u>That Should Have Been Me</u>

Echoes of applause

Fill the auditorium,

Ecstasy so pure,

And exhilaration so tangible,

The crowd roars in response.

That's me,

That will be me.

Vibrant hues

Of success, of winning,

Race across my skin.

I'm almost there,

I just know it.

Hope, desire, longing

Aches for this moment

To be mine,

Aches for me

To completely and utterly seize it.

But as the echoes, applause, and voices

Gradually die down,

A part of me is wrenched from the gaiety.

It's not me who is walking down the path

To gain omnipotence.

That's not me who is standing above all,

No, no, no,

That should have been me.

Siya Sawhney

If I Remember

If I remember hard enough

will memories that were never there

magically appear?

Will empty years

suddenly be filled with you

and will all those countless tears

never have leaked from

my jaded eyes?

If I remember hard enough

will there be an imprint of you

on the opposite side of the queen size bed?

Will we have inside jokes and remember whens

we communicate across a crowded room

and will I cease to cry

every 4th of January?

If I remember hard enough

will we be planning years ahead,

counting blessings, holding hands?

Will we not have to try so hard

to remember things that were never there?

If I remember hard enough

will you have never said goodbye?

Meg Judge

<u>Epitaphs</u>

4.23.22

I write about how

in love we were

back in our best days

I use pencil—

so tears

won't wash words away

I mean the poems

to be epitaphs

burnable ones

when it isn't enough

anymore

to say

You're dead to me

Dona McCormack

Even when I was little

I always dreamt big

Never behind

But behold

Bejewelled

Becoming

Bedazzled

Before

My kingdom was perished

Now I am just like another lost bee

Befuddled

Beleaguered

Bereft

Beyond

Isabella Quek

The Edge

Here we are once again
Standing on the doorstep of perfection
It's all too familiar
The night
The silence
Us against the world

We have been here far too many times
To know it will all be alright
In an instant it can all be taken away
The excitement
The hope
A lifetime of disappointment

When the lights go down
No one can say we didn't give our all
We left everything on the table
The promises
The dreams
Our chance to make it last

Jay Long

What if... ?

Nothing prepares you for the 'they are now engaged' notification because that's how you hear the news these days. Nothing comes at you as quickly as the 'what if' train, that hits you at such a speed you spend hours, days, weeks wondering 'what if' you had been saying goodnight all this time instead of having said that last and final goodbye.

Their quirks, their habits, their love for a certain wine, the way their smile crept up to their eyes and was always so bright that it would light up even the darkest night. Their favourite songs, their laugh, their awful hair styles will always be warm memories of being a teen and head over heels for the boy of your dreams.

You are transported right back to the weeks you spent arguing over what colour the front door would have been. All those petty arguments you had together because 'green was always more you' and 'yellow was always me' are old, distant memories. They are reminders of empty promises that were made at sixteen but the toughest one to remember is the one you both made to be married to each other before you hit your thirties.

You don't think about them much anymore, yet the notification of the occasion is a blow you'll never quite be ready for. Despite typing out 'congratulations', you're already aboard the what if train, nestled and comfortable in seat 16C but whilst reminiscing, you're still left wondering,

What if it had been me?

Meg Dring

If he truly loved my wild

IF HE TRULY LOVED MY WILD, he would have walked freely with me instead of constantly striving to fashion me into his version of what he wanted in the shadows of his mind.

IF HE TRULY LOVED MY WILD, he wouldn't project his insecurity onto me as a me problem.
Issues that were never mine to begin with somehow contributed to ammunition he would aim in my direction.

IF HE TRULY LOVED MY WILD, he wouldn't have tried to change how I love; he would remember that old souls love differently.

IF HE TRULY LOVED MY WILD, he would have known that different doesn't translate as can't be trusted. On the contrary, I was probably the most honest soul he had ever encountered.

IF HE TRULY LOVED MY WILD, then my wildest dreams would have come true, we would have been together hand in hand, heart to heart forever.

Ally Bird

<u>Elysian Fantasy</u>

With the gentle breeze blowing away,

Only traces of you remain in this sweet fantasy.

Where in search of your pieces,

I retrace our tracks to reach the place,

At which we promised to meet.

Where the sun dares not reach,

But the trees still stand guard,

Over the oath that we couldn't keep.

Even after so long lost in this distorted dream,

I still seek your presence,

And yearn for the gentle caress of your embrace,

But I can no longer find you inside my memories.

Oh, how could I?

When you now live forever in the whispers of the wind,

The song of the birds,

In the melody that echoes among the hills of this world.

You are the colors in the sky that kiss upon my skin,

And the sunshine that leaks between the leaves,

To caress my cold limbs.

Alas, time has come, to bid farewell to our past,

That is forever to be ingrained in nature's calm.

Now, it is only our traces that remain,

Among this forgotten promised land.

Meha Khan

"Goodbye to the Wishes and Dreams"

I will not wish anymore,

They've made me an errant fool.

To think that what I could wish for,

Would actually come true.

Maybe a dream is a kinder thing,

To come only when I sleep,

Vanishing before I can think,

And never mine to keep.

No, I will not think of should've,

The endings I might've had.

Do away with any could've,

The life I would've planned.

I cast them all so far away,

This weary life I'll have to embrace.

Melanie Simangan

Dreams and Stardust

She was stuck in a glass house for years,
Like the soul needed to be resurrected,
Sometimes she would burst into tears,
Unknown of the seasons passing,
She kept looking through the glass,
Wishing it might bring a new beginning.
Losing all hope, she stopped looking,
As she walked down the street,
A sweet innocent smile,
She could not help but notice,
It was like she could feel her heartbeat,
As if she woke up from years of sleep,
The sky never looked so beautiful, and the Moon shone
brightly.
It lit up the path she walked,
She had dreams like never before,
and everything was all bright around,
Every time she painted, it brought her joy,
And he fell in love with her even more.
But no one knew what was in store,
When she walked off the beaten path,
That a dragon who would bring the wrath,
She could feel the world falling apart,
Her dreams burnt into ashes,
But it was the time to go back and she must,
To chase dreams and for a new beginning
Because she was made of stardust.

Rekha Balachandran

<u>Life After Death</u>

Where do pieces of broken dreams go?
I want to go there.

To sift amongst the rubbled remains of dreams that died.

Hold them to my heart,
Resurrect them with my hands,
Bringing them back to life.

Where did the remains of burst bubbles go?
I want to go there.

Hold them to my lips,
Resuscitate them with Sacred breath,
Offering them back to the wind to ascend.

Where is this place?
Take me there.

I believe in life after death.

Monique Hemingway

Make believe

Tell me when you look at me,

What do you see?

A girl who was once a dreamer,

Who no longer believes?

Fairy tales and castles,

dragons and moats.

They were all once so vivid,

now gone up in smoke.

Imagination lost in translation,

A woman in a daze.

Fixated on growing up,

she all but lost her way.

I was once a believer

But now all I can do is stare

at picture books and stories,

Empty pages of despair.

Nicole Carlyon

Some Dreams Die

social media is a slithering prospector

unearthing gilded treasures in dreams

to market you and your precious hopes

without regard to any gems of happiness

it can dox you in its malevolent vapors

of strangulating quests—coercing you to

surrender your revered dreams and secrets

in weighty soot—smothering your truth

behind its drab escarpments of cold doubt

I was not always mindful or careful

as its minions mined doggedly to uncover

some of my secret and delicate places

even my beloved destinations of healing

which nature still struggles to protect—

to keep hidden in her sheltered stores

and in our forgotten but sacred trusts

avoid letting these emotionless machines

take advantage like it stealthily bound me

in its churn to uncover all the secreted

and delicate places of your tender heart

your extraordinary and sacred dreams

your gentle ever-flowering spirits

and every pure hope engraved in your soul

the shadows of these social tempests

can rage their darkness and inflict pain

on countless depressing hearts that weep

or absorb as good—flawed or fake realities

posted in torments of a lying pretense

built upon panoramas that appear real

while ignoring countless dreams that die

keep most of your private parts hidden—

storied away—into fables and legends

that you seal away in personal chests

buried deep in verdant protective forests

to uncover only when you need them

for your benefit or for others in want

or a loving soul kept especially for you

or the glow of your emergent posterity

protect each token of rare or golden virtue—

that defines your identity—your purpose

and ultimately—your cherished destiny

from likely assassination by the jealous

treasure up all your secret places—

into a refuge of solace where you alone

can live to tell the tales of your dreams

to empathetic ears and your true friends

obscure your most exquisite pearls

discuss your visions in a safe propriety

with your closest partner in love

your precious and wanting family

and your trees of long-deceased ancestors

friends that stand ready to release on you

fruits of their dreams and better angels

that will work relentlessly to protect

your most hallowed secrets and dreams

Doug W. Evans

Limelight

On top of the stairs, looking down at the ghosts of me, they still follow me after all these years.

I thought it would feel different, standing here where I always wanted to be, yet somehow, I can't ignore this pervasive emptiness taking over me. And I wish I could go back to the safety of the past, where daydreams were made of rose gold clouds and butterflies. Where you and I were still meant to be, talking about escaping to the jungle where the humid air would make our hair curly. It feels so lonely here without you at the finish line, and I wonder if I lived on misplaced desires all along. My mistakes feel heavy now.

Blinded by the limelight, I lost sight of your face, I only held onto my Dolce & Gabbana shades and my fake smile. There is no going back now. I can only hope to find you again by a miracle, in a time loop, where the warped paths of our souls meet again. Because with all that I gained, losing you was not worth it.

Olivia Bella

Daydreams & Lost Wishes

She always dreamt of being a doctor,

To lend a helping hand to those in need.

Wished to be one amongst those with a white coat and a stethoscope,

Helping people heal and making people believe in miracles.

Not knowing the repercussions of wanting to follow her dream,

She continued, and yearned to someday achieve it.

But life had other plans.

The dreams she had been dreaming to live,

Were crushed into pieces.

The decision for her life was made,

By someone who assured it to be for her best.

That day, she cried to let go of her wishes,

And compromised herself, for wanting something badly.

Yet she smiles today to hide her pain,

For broken dreams and lost wishes hurt the most.

She continues to be as kind and compassionate as she can be,

To help people heal,

Maybe not through medicines, but definitely through her words.

Prachi Singh

December

The sky looks down with sombre eyes.

The hearth is empty, the ember sighs.

I am cold since last December,

Though you may not remember.

The windows rattle, the door's ajar.

The cold creeps in and touches the scar

which you gave me last December,

Though you may not remember.

In the backyard, I see roses wilt,

The dream in crumbles which I built.

I pick the debris of December,

Though you may not remember.

RS

The Corpse Bride

His words dripped sweet, like nectar;
Tales of tulips, love, and forever;
Coated promises of a future together.

Elaborate lies.

Without warning, he was gone – promising that same forever
to another.

Leaving her with nothing but shattered remnants of a
disillusioned reality,
a very broken heart, and the stench of rotting tiger lilies whose
sickly-sweet smell burned her nostrils...

Forever entombing love's effigy inside her heart.

Valerie Leyden-Morffi

Gathering Pieces

Dreams flowed like fresh spring water

when my soul was tender to the touch ...

when I was younger, thinner,

less exhausted, more inspired,

and ferociously convinced

that the misguided fantasies

of possibility

were nothing more

than friendly visitors to welcome

with smooth ivory hands

and lanky open arms

(never wolves in sheep's clothing).

Limitlessness was my mantra

and I was the fledgling lioness,

hunting for a life bigger

than what's granted to

a waitress and a wife.

(I would become

everything they weren't

and anything

they didn't believe I could be …

until settling into the red flags,

birthing hips,

extinguished lips,

embarrassed smile,

and freshly broken home

with melting complacency.

It was simpler before the cracks

bled my spirit dry.)

In this life, I'll never be

a paleontologist or astronaut,

Egyptologist or anthropologist.

Instead, shattered fragments

are assembled anew

to rise from the fractures

as a version of myself

that I never imagined becoming —

complete, unknown,

and entirely whole.

Renée Novosel

<u>Ad Astra</u>

Broken teenagers, shattered dreams,

Counting to the farewell.

I hope you know, you had me at hello.

Bury our deepest despairs, save the tears, together.

Your hazel eyes are love reincarnated,

I lose myself in its depths.

These screaming voices say,

I'm unworthy of your gaze.

Sculpting my fears so I can break them,

Your fingers drew constellations on the nape of my neck.

Made of glass, now with a purpose.

Tell me how it feels to have a heartbeat.

Even if the end comes early,

Until the world falls away,

I carve this space for you out of myself.

Love me in lavender, so will I.

For the ocean has the moon,

And I have you.

Nikitha Senny

Lights Out

She used to sleep in the city,

Bathing in the soft glow of street lamps,

The buzz that follows you home,

The hum of a beating heart.

But she woke up this morning

In her sunken childhood bed,

Stuck in a ghost town,

With a silence she couldn't stand.

Her city's trapped in a $3 frame

Next to a jar of pennies, half empty.

She can still see herself in the jungle

But secretly she knows,

She'll never touch the concrete.

Rozalyn Walton

Nothing Comes

I wish to fall gracefully from my own weeping world.
I wish to shatter, not in bits and pieces,
but wholly and messy. I want my fall to be loud.
I want for every bone to break as loud
as anything can be. I wish to be heard.
And very secretly, I wish to be embraced.

I want for the sky to look down to me.
For it to nod and gently scrub the ache
from my cheeks as it falls with me.

And within the undoing of all the ache
I had to muster in order for my fall to happen,
I want to be understood.

And if anything in the world will understand,
it is thunder. It is rain. It is nature.

And yet I sit here. With wrists still stretched out.

Reaching for an answer from a world that does not listen.

My world brims with emotion, but whenever asked
for a solution to all of this, my world stands still
and freezes. It waits with me.

But nothing comes.

S.A. Quinox

pull back memories

i cast my net on the edge of the sea,

so to pull back memories.

a life now gone not out of mind,

a world more sweet and kind.

children playing in the streets,

care not they to win the feats.

mudpies made on rainy days,

schools closed on snow days.

a life carefree not so bogged down,

there seemed more time to get around.

there be now more advances than before,

yet a simpler life disappears behind closed doors.

Amanda Thuy

<u>Wish Upon A Fallen Star</u>

As the day became an antonym,

she stood there on her balcony.

The sky above her twinkled,

lit with stars burning in agony.

Reminiscing about her

now broken dreams,

a lone tear crossed the

threshold of her eye;

mimicking the action of that tear,

a twinkling star fell from the sky.

Lost in the abyss were her wishes

once woven by her heart

and the star falling from the sky

was the one she used to wish upon.

Her dreams fell out of her heart

while the star fell from its grace.

Why did it happen?

No one could explain.

What once were burning

desires of her heart

Daydreams & Lost Wishes

are now the epitaphs

of those wishes lost!

R.Z.O'Connor

DROWNING WISHES

Today was a fairy-tale moment

You are there in my heart

Lingering in every breath

Flying with my hopes

Living in my dreams

I was caught in an illusion

Dancing with angels

Thinking you were real

Entangled in fantasies

Giving hope to

My drowning wishes

In my faltering fantasies

Your fluttering

Captivating my heart

Sabotaging my sweet love

Stealing my deepest desires

Killing my innocent soul ....

Saiqah Salim

The Beach

One day, I was asked,

If you could go, anywhere in the world. Where would you be
right now?

In an innocent half-truth, I said,

At the beach.

But on that day,

I wanted to be where you were.

Lost in the Universe that is you,

Found in the arms you fold around me,

Watching the Sun's bed hair peak out on the horizon.

But. I lied.

Because I can't.

So, I smiled,

And in an innocent half-truth I said,

At the beach...

JustSammy

Daydreams & Lost Wishes

I don't want you here
I like you gone
When the only you is one of my imagination

I hold conversations in my head
Weave fantasies of your return
It's a fiction I can hide in

Lying close to the truth
Inspired by real life
Glimpses drawn of a future to the fullness of its possibility

You return
And with the opening of a door
The dream closes

Illusions disintegrating
Fading from memory
Like whispered promises.

Adeola Sheehy

WHAT WAS NEVER REAL

How do I move on from what was never real?

Though your infinite light, indeed, is true,

how much time must pass for fantasy to heal?

As joyous it was, once, to feel,

it becomes hard when there's nothing to lose.

How do I move on from what was never real?

Hoping sweetly for the grand reveal,

or confession to never come from you.

How much time must pass for fantasy to heal?

My heart was yours, you saw, to steal,

but was not a thought for you to choose.

How do I move on from what was never real?

Invention, oft, is my ideal—

this time it's spent me through and through.

How much time must pass for fantasy to heal?

I prayed for truth in the surreal,

instead finding myself of little value.

How do I move on from what was never real?

How much time must pass for fantasy to heal?

Sammy T. Anderson

Do you remember?

Do you remember

The first night that we met?

How your eyes glistened

like the moonlit sky

on a clear autumn night.

How our voices converged

to form an arrangement of sounds.

Echoing in a rhythmic display,

creating sparks

that exploded into fireworks

as soon as we kissed.

Do you remember

our first fight?

Where our voices screamed out

of disarrangement,

splattering against our hearts.

Leaving black paint where scarlet

would shine.

Little did we know that the black

would convert

into a strong palace gate

that no intruder could destroy.

Do you remember

the first time we had sex?

Where are bodies finally aligned.

Feeling your heavy breath on my

Chest.

Savoring the feel of your hands,

scratching their way down my back,

carving into words the feelings

that filled my mind.

Do you remember

the first time I said I love you,

the words

choking my throat?

Turning blue from the nervousness

of waiting for you to say the words

back.

You did.

Without hesitation,

without fear.

Do you remember

when we broke down

on the side of the highway

on that cold winter's night?

Tires frosted over,

Sliding,

racing without control,

plunging

into the depths.

But, there you were.

Able to carry me out from the

shadows.

Out of the wreckage

of what I thought was my heart.

Fearing that I'd lose you forever.

Do you remember that night,

where you said you'd be back

324

in a couple of hours or so?

Leaving me to my anxious thoughts,

battering my mind.

Blunt force trauma knocking me cold,

or was it the drink in my hands

that was practically gone?

Laying on the floor,

I dreamed of a nightmare,

the one where I lost

everything I held dear.

My shining star,

my guiding light.

The one who tied my soul

to theirs with an invisible string.

The tension pulling us close.

But,

it had snapped.

That's when it happened.

When your body laid close to

Another.

Daydreams & Lost Wishes

Kissing the places

where my lips once met.

Laying their hands

on your warm skin,

where I once laid my hands.

Feeling the sense of euphoria.

The feeling that I no longer had.

Do you remember

the morning after,

where you said,

We need to talk?

Telling me our fortress has collapsed,

that you've been feeling this way

for weeks.

I was no longer entrusted

with your heart in my hands.

You said you felt alone,

that you handed me the bricks,

a foundation to build upon.

But, every time I laid a brick,

it was in the wrong direction.

Wrong placement.

And I would try again

with no prevail.

You said you felt

like you had no hand to grasp

if you fell from the tower.

Hastily constructed,

with the bricks that laid

with no mortar

to hold them together,

and, in that tower

housed our feelings

in a jar.

That jar had shattered.

My fragments of myself

scattered to the floor.

Each shard,

memories seem to be casted.

Alone.

And in one of those fragments,

Daydreams & Lost Wishes

I saw my soul

turning from a scarlet red of passion

to a ghostly white of snow.

That's when I knew.

Maybe soul mates,

which I once thought were true,

turned out to be a hoax,

a scam,

a myth.

I thought my soul mate was you.

Little did I know,

soul mates

were too good to be true.

Seth Duval

IV

drip   drip   drip

I watch as it feeds me
   in this now vacant room
      a reflection of myself
      the vacancy that's crept
   it's way into me
   year after year
      until it's consumed
      my very being

drip   drip   drip

I watch
   realizing I'm just biding time
      keeping myself from dying
      while knowing I will
   never truly live again
drip   drip   drip

Daydreams & Lost Wishes

It's lonely here

in this place

where my soul

used to be

a void remains

she is gone

the girl with the

boundless energy and

unwavering determination

she's tired   so very tired

I mourn for her

her spirit

her joy

I mourn for the life that was lost

that no one else knows

is gone

Shelley Sanders-Gregg

<u>Mourning you</u>

I'm beginning to come to terms

with what life chose for me

that dreams don't always come true

and you will never be with me

I mourn this dream

it was the best I ever had

so soft and sweet

a spider's web reflecting in the sunshine

There's so much I love about you

and I wanted the chance

to always be next to you

to keep you safe

and understand you when nobody does

I wanted to devote part of my life to holding space for you

I wanted to see you in the mornings and in the evenings

I wanted to know about your every day

to catch every little change

Daydreams & Lost Wishes

to know your every dream

I wanted to show you all of me too

I wanted to build trust so deep

that we'd be safer with each other than alone

I wanted to see you grow old

hold your aged shaking hand

And when the world would become so different we would no longer understand it

that's when we'd understand each other the best

Now it dawns on me that we will never be that

not to each other

Yes, we'll always be close

I hope with all my heart

but I won't see you sleep and won't see you wake up

There will be parts of you that will never be for me

parts I'll never get to touch nor see

Somebody else will be the love of your life

I hope she'll love you fully

Daydreams & Lost Wishes

gently and kindly

she'll be able to hold you when you can't

she'll keep you safe

and will always be on your side

And I hope you'll love someone the way I loved you

it's a precious light in the dark

it kept me alive when I almost couldn't go on

It reminded me of the magic in the world

it was my hope, my safe space, my lighthouse

It scares me to let this go

I don't know what to hold on to in my moments of sorrow

I held on to you for all these years

Will I ever find another I would love as easily as I loved you?

There was no effort, no trying

I always just loved you

through all the moments

at times against my will

I loved you through my fears and wounds

nothing made that light weaker

Daydreams & Lost Wishes

I never before nor after felt that way

Just the memory of you in my head made everything brighter

But I want to give my heart to a person

one day, when I'll know myself enough

after I'll live all my adventures

and the time will slow down

I want to connect my soul to another

And now that I know it can't be you

I'm mourning you

Shireen (Širín Ježková)

Blindsided

Exhilaration

Raced up my skin,

Just the thought

Of

Winning,

Of

Climbing

Higher than anyone's expectations were,

Was beyond

Exciting.

Such anticipation

And

Ecstasy,

Over all that could happen,

Collided with everything else in my mind.

I was blindsided

By something I thought

Would let me breathe in the same colors

Daydreams & Lost Wishes

I was never able to see

How can I yearn for something that I never quite had in the first place?

Why does my heart ache for the exhilaration that got lost amidst it all?

Why does the entirety of my existence

Long for another chance,

Another opportunity,

Anything, absolutely anything.

Siya Sawhney

A Mother's Lost Wish

Two lines on the stick,

Enormous smile on my lips.

Hands sliding through belly,

One two hundred times already.

Dreaming of gender,

Have everything surrendered

To a tiny life inside,

Who bought us so much delight.

Daydreaming about being a mother rest of the life,

Making each day glad of being alive.

I saw him on the screen, yes 'him'.

Desperately wishing to hold him in my arms

And calling me mom.

Selected thousands of names,

Awaiting for his movements to capture in the frame.

I have this beauty glow on my face,

Can do anything, everything for his embrace.

They planned a baby shower.

There I was in a blue dress with flower.

When suddenly everything went black and I fell on my back,

Just to wake up with a flat tummy.

Milestones away from the word mummy.

Tears never leaving my eyes,

Now that I am surrounded by stormy skies.

I fell from the sky bridge,

Crushed my bones on the pavement.

I decorated with the lost wish.

All that remain is a hope

That someday I will be at the end of this slope.

Sneha Sagare

Numbness (we can't recover from)

We were a collision all over again.
A beautiful crash with bursting stars and every time we collided,
we created new galaxies.
In your eyes, I can see constellations that turn us in a cosmic
storm,
One we can't recover from.
We're creating worlds in dimensions
parallel to universes that only we discover in the void above.
Our presence illuminates an aurora.
We, however, are en perfect eclipse,
Hidden behind noctilucent clouds.

————————————————

My heart is raised by the thought
that every step I take is one towards you.
The strange feeling in my stomach
is one between nausea and adrenaline.
A warmth that lingers somewhere between my ribs and my
thighs.
And a fear in my spine that needs a firm hand and hungry eyes.
I have thoughts about what was and what is.
What can be or might never come.
An insecurity that clasps its claws in my ankles.
A quarrion in my chest that flickers lightly but burns a hole that
feels like the blisters on my heart.
One that has been hurt so many times.
It still holds courage to give you the benefit of the doubt.
Trust issues between stuttering words,
and flutters of hope on the wings that I grew every time I bite
my tongue.
The anticipation that lingers on my lips.
Those that taste so sweet when they meet yours.

And I fall, all over again.

The lump of fear that's residing in my chest fills up an entire desert full of resentment.
The tears behind my eyes could fill an ocean that isn't from this world.
I silence my words as I walk through the hallways of regret.
And I numb the anger every time I close the doors of pain.
I shut the windows to my heart and barricade to a point of no return.
I peel off my skin and rip out my tongue.
I don't feel the need to spill the words that poison the dirt I crawl on.
I suffocate on the toxic waste that resembles my existence.
I'd rather die in the abyss with my soul.

Stephanie Haveman

"Missed Opportunity"

When she was born, that was your chance
to express your love with more than a glance.
A time for your soul to seek redemption –
to receive an informal rite of exemption
from being judged by my inner child.
To prevent your heart from being exiled
from my life completely; banished for good.
Any past mistakes would've been understood
if only you tried to open your eyes,
acknowledge my struggle and realize
the damage you've caused; the emotional pain.
Your newfound vision could've helped you regain
the trust that was lost, repairing my core shame.
Sadly, you refuse to accept any blame;
choosing to live with your unwavering stance,
that young me never needed more than a glance.

T.B. Elden

LOVE LIKE WINTER

At first
like the sun
that stole a frigid frost.
Toasty
like the marshmallows
we melted over fire.
Fresh like peppermint
wrapped in candy cane stripes.
Abundant
with earthy warm spiced goodness.
And sweet
with sprinkles of bitter notes
like burnt molasses.

Then silent
as the cold
unsympathetic air
that drilled through
our bones.
Like tormented toes
that trudged through
foot deep snow.
Empty;
golden autumnal
magic
stripped for barren
arms
where hugs were
strangers.

That was us
we lit and died like splinters.
Enchanting but desolate
our love like winter

Stuti Sinha

Threadbare

Trying on an old me,
from the back of the wardrobe,
amid mothballs and dust,
to see if I still fit.
A patchwork in varying shades
of the once familiar.

Loose now, on the shoulders
and tight across the chest.
A cozy, time-worn collar
turned up against chill winds.
A stranger's narrow arms
which held on far too long.

Lint-strewn pockets,
threadbare with memories
of warmth and clumsy fingers
on lazy autumn evenings.
Tucked inside, a creased old wish,
tattered by forgotten storms.
A yearning for a life
never quite within reach.

This wish never fit right,
even when I wanted it.
I tuck it back away,
in a pocket sized tomb,
put the old me away
to languish in dust.

I have newer clothes
to wear now.

Xan Indigo

I strum my silver saudade

As the sky drapes its skin over the land
Laced with a sheening tinge
Strings like veins in form of silver bands
Tethered my heart with a fatal cinch.
Around my ankles they fetter,
Till my soul can't shift a single inch.
I fall back.

I love, I love,
I love like these unbreakable strings.
Silver smooth delicate guitar strings
Follow wherever my loves wander to.
And as I strum, a saudade they'd soulfully sing
"love loves longing and love's a beautiful thing"
Strings swathe me with a swaddle
And tell me what they've hurt would heal,
Yet how strings strangle is all I feel,
And this suffocating dream
That strives to
Kill.

Karen Chan

<u>Nothing at All</u>

I feel raw
Like a wound freshly scraped…sensitive to every passing breath
Moments falling like icicles…piercing the unreal silence of
thoughts
Tides of time washing over me…crushing my soul
Changing seasons hurling me around…scorching, biting,
bruising my mind
I feel so much…and yet…nothing at all
You took my reds and my blues…and left NOTHING AT ALL

Swati Upadhyay

<u>Write about you</u>

I'm driving away on a road with no end
Remind me of the roads I no longer see
Remind of people I no longer know
Wonder if you remember those times with me
If you think of me when you drive away
The times you drove away with me

Why, what seemed enough yesterday
Is suddenly not today
I always knew it would be tough
And by the way
I never said you could stay
It was already late that day
I felt like you had to repay

Such a stupid soul
Full of hope
On someone she never knew
If only I knew by then
It probably wouldn't change a thing
Since what I feel is always stronger than what I know

What I know about you
Is what I used to
Now you're a shadow
Walking away from me
and the only thing I can do
Is write about you

I feel nostalgic tonight
Suddenly I can recall all the good times

Daydreams & Lost Wishes

For long I thought they were erased from my mind
I think this might be the night that I forgive you
And this makes me realize
That all our past was not a waste of time

Tayane de Oliveira

Baking Bad

There's a recipe unique
to each emotion –
and we can vary the
ingredients each round.

Tonight's sadness is thick –
equal parts
loss and defeat –
stir through some
disappointment and add
in a sprinkle of frustration.

It is bitter and it's dense –
and my mind cannot
stop kneading it,
asking what does
this actually need??

And there is no answer.
There is just a broken oven
to bake it till it burns.
Once it's black I can
discard the failure –
maybe cook up something
different in the morning.

Tiffany O'Brien

<u>Atlas</u>

Why didn't I get an atlas?

I don't know how to navigate roads that are not on any map.

Alleys, dirt roads, pebbled paths, the side of a mountain ...?

All places my heart has traveled.

When visions of an Olympic medal died ...

When dreams of motherhood died ...

When a marriage died.

A part of me died with each ending.

Then people I love so deeply died.

Parts of my soul stop breathing.

How does this body carry so much loss and still live?

I could die too.

It is an option.

An option I considered a time or two.

But no, no, I won't give in to that taunting.

My soul still has breath and dreams and love.

I see a rainbow after a smack down of a thunderstorm.

I see my geese do a fly over in impossible weather.

I stand on a shore of a vast ocean and my soul feels alive ...
again.

Those little simple things remind me ... I am still here.

I am here for a reason.

A purpose that keeps evolving.

An atlas won't help.

In fact it might confuse matters.

I'm learning to sit still and let my soul feel the presence of

great grace one moment at a time.

Never fully knowing where the next turn of a corner will take

me.

But trusting in a Higher Power that divinely orchestrates the
symphony of my life.

Melissa Nickert

So near, yet so far.

To transverse to a place of peace
Where, in your gaze, I find my home.
Your tenderness creates for me a breeze
And in your dreams I roam;

To let my soul finally become alive
So that in your love I can thrive,
I'd fill your day with laughter
For you I'd chase away the clouds of grey.
I'd stay lovingly by your side for many years;

Yet here we are, defeated today,
So near yet so far,
In a place where we can't stay,
So near yet so far.

I'd let my smile brighten your day,
My tears wash away your fears,
For happiness with you is homemade
Thus from my face I remove this masquerade.

To rest my head on your shoulder
And leave the worries that I carry,
For life is what is seen by the beholder
But in this journey, one cannot be unwary;

As here we are defeated today
So near yet so far,
In a place where we can't stay,
So near yet so far.

Umme Huzayfah

Noceuse

The wind howled outside, rattling the windows.

Darkness. A lighter spark.

She inhales and looks at the clock – 2:13am.

She waved her white flag to Mistress Insomnia long ago.
This was when her mind became most active, and the seeded
feeling of loneliness took root, sprouting through her core.

Lighter spark. Candle lit.

She catches a glimpse of her reflection in the window...
Weary-eyed and wisps of grey now infiltrating her raven hair.

If only time would slow down for just a bit. Just a moment.
It only speeds up with each passing day.

The loneliness spreads.

Haunted by the ghost of Him (her angel, equally her nightmare)
she begins to doubt if she'll ever find true love... reciprocated
love.

Bottle open. Drink poured.

She takes a swig and swallows. That comforting warmth glides
smoothly down her throat, spreading throughout her body.

Lighter spark.

She exhales, extinguishing the candle.

Darkness.

The wind continues to rattle the windows as she takes another sip... 2:57am.

Valerie Leyden–Morffi

the rain and the wind

the rain slips out of her dress

she gathers all of the sharp things
with a fullness swelling

hauntingly and tragically
she wells in his eyes
trickling softly
finding the plum of his throat

she wants to do to him what autumn
does to the fallow earth floor

carrying a scorched tongue
she arranges herself along the riverbed
all stained knees and pebbly cuts

oh, please take this weight
and endure me

for the rain knows she could wash away
the sins and sighs

Daydreams & Lost Wishes

and if she closes her eyes
she can almost hear
the wind whip her hair
tightly around his fist,
clutched and begging for wear

arms outstretched, she falls
into this river forged before her

an eternal thirst acquiesced,
impalpably so

Kelsey Singh

Wishes Lost

They dance into the distance,
wishes lost on the
autumn breeze,
and I cling onto the remnants,
but they slip away
with ease,
and I sit in
sorrowful silence,
conjuring hopes that
never last,
and I know it
must be my fault
for the traumas I suffered
in the past
that haunt me
with an intensity
that will repeat itself
again and again,
unless I forgive myself
for my transgressions,
and eradicate the shame—

for there is always
the chance to move on,
with the opportunity
to change.

J. Sexton

Passion, Pain, Purpose

The deepest of pain reveals a calling on the other side.

Heart so heavy

it physically hurts to breath. Blindsided

by rage and words.

I go back in time

to sweet love.

Notes, names and nuances of deep intimacy.

But recalling that makes my chest and gut hurt more.

The volume and outburst of callous and cruel verbage echos.

Yet I go silent

amidst fear and confusion.

Where once I felt so safe

and sure of my future.

I now face a deep chasm of unknown. It would seem

I know you not.

I gather courage to ask questions. Met with silence.

I must now find my own answers. This calling becomes a quest

that is met by the fierce Phoenix rising within me.

Melissa Nickert

The World

The sky is vivid, with swirling circles and
tender flashes of intermittent sparkle.
In this world, you can be who you wish.

Today I choose to sit.
I sit most days, and look over the vast mountain range,
the several setting suns, and I draw.

I draw a picture of me, a picture of who I think I should be.
This world is full of pleasure and delight, but this picture
draws from me a fright.

An inner truth, far from my own.
Something in this picture wishes to be shown,
but I draw, and I gaze, gaze in bliss, oh what more have I to
wish?

In this world, there are grey trees that wind forever,
with small, thin, clear branches growing high over hill,
and a persistent chime, a ring of a bell.
There is a daily update, a kind voice in my ear. She tells me
things,
my heart holds dear. Little trinkets of things that don't make
much sense,

but my eyes fill, and body tense.

I'm happy here, I wake each day,
I wake with a thirst for life, and a zest for its way.
Each day is different, but also the same.

A day that's healthy, calm, and tame,
but today I woke up to the sound of clatter,
the ground beneath me cracked. I fell.

Into darkness I was thrown, into a world, I think was known?
A woman stood over me, her voice familiar,
I smile with glee.

Kerryanne Brown

Galaxy Brain

We are born in incomprehensible slow motion, under a sky
pregnant with the swell of rain
as we're dropped mercilessly onto the skin of this wailing speck
of a planet
screaming at one another from the moment we draw breath.

I'm baby-faced and naive at eighteen, with eyes that don't yet
know the darkness, standing on the lip of a bowl of stars at the
cusp of womanhood, bright-eyed, in my babydoll dress and
butterfly clips—
but the constellations inexorably fall from my laurel crown, one
by one.

I shove time into a bottle, lidded with a childproof cap, and I'm
eighty pounds heavier—
the burden of biology and decades of self-destruction, topped
with a pandemic just to add flair, draped from an image I no
longer recognize

I'm wrapped in a flimsy sheet as reassuring as the gasp of
hemoglobin soaking through it,
spilling from my unfed neurons, the color of tar and sprinkled
with a galaxy of stars suddenly lost…
I had so much hope in daydreams and wishes.

And in everything blurred across my vision, dragging down a
mirror with no jagged edges,
because sometimes night falls and doesn't stop unraveling,
the yellow of the moon shivering into gravity.

And all that's left of me is cracked, gray and drab, warped and
twisted, like a surrealist painting–
when the color drains from the world and is left swirling in a
hyper-pigmented mass,
swallowed up by a hole at my feet like bathwater, my spine
sticking out like a hackled nerve.

My flesh is no longer my own–but smudged onto someone
else's canvas,
where I am more acceptable, bite-sized, and easier to manage
and people like me who are square pegs can be arranged as they
please.

I cut my spirit out when I sold my soul to escape hypoxia,
because when you're "too sensitive"
and "too soft", it's like they're dirty words or slow diseases they
might catch,
their white, manicured hands suffocating you from behind as
they shame you
for pressing your fingers into the earth so that you can feel it
breathe.

And later, I start to believe the disease is actually a lesion carved
somewhere through my gray matter, siphoned away into a
gravitational singularity, where I'm collapsing inside my own
darkness,
as my soul staggers towards the brink of tomorrow.

There's a howling void in my mind, hanging bare like a door
that once led me *home*,
ripped from its hinges—and the rainbow of color has all gushed
out like blood,
because there is no room for it in this world.

Everything is Instagram perfect, white picket fences, gray walls,
designer bags that all look identical,
even though you're told to "be yourself!" but they all whisper a
dialect that's foreign to me
as they're outside scrubbing their shutters with a toothbrush in
this gated community, where no one can have broken windows
or misshapen hedges, or wildflowers growing out of their ears.

And those who hold that chromatic galaxy within their brains
can never feel at ease...
but if we would just lay *still*, allow our breath to fall soft,
we would see how we glint and shimmer in the path of the
moon.

In this realm language is our salvation, how we rid ourselves of
our shadows,
but as the world exists– words are torn from my mouth,
useless birds that rise and vanish with no translation.

Screamed into the sterile halls of my synapses, where i exist as
the gilded,
paradoxal allegory of both [--*agoraphobia and claustrophobia*—]
and as I bludgeon my own spirit in the prison of my mind for
things I cannot control
in a world fresh out of empathy for the externalized noise in
your brain—

Who should be left with the burden of me, touch-starved flesh
and yet volatile recluse?
any shred of warmth or friendship, and I devour it until there is
nothing left to be given.

Like a fire that has gone inverted, drenched in what I took too much of—
too intense. too emotional. too broken.
how many more sectors of me must die before i am allowed to live? how long can i stand the dark
before I morph and bleed into the shadows, my eyes haunted by the bones of past versions of myself?

As mammals, we're afraid we'll be caught in the cold blue of winter, but what if we would accept falling as snowflakes?
splintered shards forking and branching off of one another, no two the same, swallowing starlight of celestial birds—and not worrying about being accepted, or squawking with hollow tongues,

Afraid of obtuse faces in a world where white earbuds are a status symbol,
and Starry Night is on everything, but no one knows the brilliant anguish of the man behind it,
and how the faceless ones forced him into the silence of the water as well.

But I remember, as I unclench myself and let love reclaim my body— even the rainbow
hides its splendor until after the storm, and as I pull the darkness tangled in my dendrites out by the roots, playing tug of war with my own etymology, shaking off the matted earth—

That I've been given a pen.

…and the universe upheaves everything i've ever known by pulling me through a mirror, my image shattering from my ill-formed preconceptions, bending time, droplets bleeding

together in deferred, spectral, synchronous parallax, in a blurred
glimmer like diffraction,

When light bends as it enters my eye, creating a halo,
rewriting my life in the most inconceivable mythology
and the gasping, stuttering syntax of my once muted heart once
again *drinks starlight*,
the cobwebs in corners of my mind IGNITE into star nurseries,
and I remember:

*I am not from this realm, my skin smells of the sky and is clouded
with nebulae,
and as I busy myself transmuting past pain into passion, i will no
longer compete with sharp voices,
and when chaos speaks my name, instead i'll soak my mind in
prismatic waters instead of your
darkened perception of the ghost in my rear-view mirror that you still
want me to be.*

Lauren Lee Verse

Daydreams & Lost Wishes

I am a landscape drawn like a map of turmoil, of a dream lost in the warren of who I am, I wonder...

I once had ribbon-shaped rivers of yearning that flowed generously within me because they attested to a sovereignty of their own; bending and turning vigorously like an unbound spirit; unleashed and untamed. But they seized to run freely long ago. They shrunk, twisted into a silent strip, a shallow creek without power or essence. Merely gurgling helplessly, ineffective, ebbing quietly into indiscernible drips.

Much like the dream I once harboured of conquering the world with my wit, travelling the borders of this stunning earth and soaking in its colours until I was a palette of self-made beauty. I would become a nomad of a temporary realm. Alas, I was fooling only me.

I have become surrounded with borders made of steep mountains, chaining their way around my heart. They much resemble a birdcage barring all fleeting, inane emotions, strictly reminding me of all things expected. But these boundaries were not always so daunting, alas, once they were but frontiers made by rows of red-seeded dandelions, floating away with a breath ever so light. I was made silly from an innocence harboured for too long until a merciful truth shook me into place; travel the world? Dreams are for cowards, I was told. Not by a voice; but by my own ingrained self-doubt.

These mountains claim to protect me with subtle severity; it is much better to stay shackled than to swallow the truth of being a nomad of failures merely; even if the truth arrives as a merciful burst of rain to parched lips.

And so, I still wait behind rocky walls. I am still searching to find the roots which will keep me steady; lift me beyond the bulwark even if it is too late. I still have my hands deep in the barren soil, fumbling for the tangible answer to a lingering dream;

did I merely lose my way between who I was and who I wanted to be, or did I perish somewhere in between?

Saba Ahmed

[regret]

ri-gret / *noun*

These fine shards of hope will remain scattered like a broken mirror of lost dreams and we must tread carefully for they cut deep, so we trace our fingers around the soft-winged silhouettes of our words that used to give such comfort; alas, we have become numb, lost in a meadow of promises where each syllable once was a tender whisper and now bursts forth like a crescendo amid a funeral; how very burlesque we have become in our need to have more than mere blueprints of regret on our ribs; to be more than dreams lost and pledges broken; we cannot wash away the grief even with a flood of remorse.

Saba Ahmed

Shelters

The house:
crumbles, bright siding
warps, weathered and worn,
no longer recognizable.
Its heart—the family within—
moves somewhere
with automated everything.

Where:
"wear" means fading and holes
to fabric and clothes,
replaceable things, and not
the slow breaking down of
the family's soul.

The home:
no thing of stone or wood
but muscle and blood,
which shelters like the dome
of a magnificent oak—from
the mighty center of many arms.

Dona McCormack

METAPHORS TO DESCRIBE MY HEART

1. Something of a lost cause in the wrong hands.
2. A music player with a faulty key playing the same sad tune over again.
   Over again.
3. A treacherous winding pathway in the form of too much forgiveness.

If you hold it true to your ear, you can hear it,
the waves,
the broken promises escaping with the wind,
a cacophony of deafening want and unsteady beats.
Well wishes as their back turned upon me.

If you listen closely –
there will be but a single moment of calm,
where the love sits, patiently,
relentless in almost acceptance.

Shaye Wallace

I am tired.

I am tired of writing letters to my vulnerability,

my ink weeps on paper,

but at one point my words try to abruptly end the show,

and I am left with an incomplete poem.

incomplete poems stand in a waitlist,

waiting to feel whole,

tired eyes droop and they are left astray on an open road.

I feel sorry for them but I can't come up with things to write,

and that's a poet's biggest fear,

when you wake up one day and the curtains of the world are

down,

what can you do now?

Tejasvee Nagar

<u>Acception</u>

Reaching for those wildflower wishes,

Only to be enticed by the whisper in the window.

One fleeting moment and everything fades away.

Warned before, yet embraced the dark

And now folded in all the wrong places.

To the ones who left your heart by the door,

My eyes were all for those shining lies.

I'm sorry, I never saw you.

My heart may be doomed, my mind cursed,

Can it be undone, the damage caused?

You don't want to know what called me,

The echoes in the forest, don't listen to them.

After the thunderstorms,

Say hello to the moon for me, will you?

Nikitha Senny

I'm here again, it's as though I never truly leave. Unbothered and unafraid, I get to exist in this realm of endless peace. It's a beautiful thing, to be able to bring yourself into this place; all you have to do is silence your eyes. Let the weight of it all surround you like the heaviest of blankets and the warmest embrace. Soon the dark will become light and you create this sphere to carry your soul, far beyond any ache your little fragile heart knows. The stillness becomes ethereal. The wounds you carry heal.

But what comes must also go and the light will soon dim again. The sunshine will be drained of its life and we must return to this reality we orbit, crawling back into our unfortunate truths.

Not to forget this field of dreams is but a blink away from nightmares, you must pick where and when. You'll find out soon, just watch and wait until your eyes grow silent yet again.

Victoria Jay

Daydreams & Lost Wishes

We will meet once more

without the apprehension of a *goodbye*,

under a broken sky,

with bruised kisses

and crushed bones.

Now, a hush of knowing falls,

the stars misalign,

the night air reverberates it

like an e c h o

from some unknown place

in the cosmos.

Every river, every mountain,

every particle of stardust aching

before it ever reaches

the beat of your heart.

R. Deshea Poetry

<u>Young Love</u>

Middle school, mood swings

Strawberry lipstick in early spring

His smirky face, hazel eyes

Looking directly in mine

I ignored the first time

But I couldn't stop thinking

How he and I fit like a perfect rhyme

Bicycle rides, brushing hands

Dancing on our favorite bands

Kissing behind the mall

Spending hours on call

We felt like a movie leads

Like Noah and Allie

We could be a happy family

Get married, have kids and die casually

Be there for each other in heaven and hell

Keep on day dreaming till we hear the bell

Daydreams & Lost Wishes

But as they say young love don't always last forever

Circumstances couldn't keep us together

The transfer came in dead center

I guess our story was never meant to be in the notebook

Just to meet and never to be

With you I lost half of me

We never said our last byes

Didn't have the courage to see the broken heart

Or perhaps we hoped of meeting again with a restart

Sneha Sagare

L o o k F o r C l o u d N u m b e r 9

I whispered in the moon's ear so she could send you my words tonight. But your curtains are drawn, and your windows are suddenly shut closed.

And so I waited—night; after night; after night.

I sent you small pieces of myself wrapped in music, in hopes you would leave the keys under your Welcome Home mat.

But more nights went by, and each one grew quiet and longer.

So to pass the time, I began hopping from one lonely cloud to the next, also to see if I'd be lucky enough to land in a puddle of rain.

I thought to myself, "What did you misplace this time?"

But I was sure you wouldn't forget me.

Right?

Still, I threw tiny paper planes to knock for me. I've scribbled pieces of myself just in case you remember to miss me. I've gathered hummingbirds and butterflies even though I know I'm too heavy for them to fly. You see, love is always worth a try, especially when you know what you'll be losing. So please don't make me lose it all. You're all I have.

There are some nights I feel your tears on my cheeks. I know when your eyes are sad, as I've seen them too many times. Do you feel the same way too?

I grew helpless but always hopeful. You taught me how to dream once more, to be wishful again.

Although nights went on and I just knew...

It's sad that we're running out of time. It's sadder that it just keeps on going.

But that's okay.

I'll try to find my way back to you. Besides, home is wherever we make it to be.

So, before we totally drift apart,

I'll leave this prayer in the cloud where I waited the longest. Open it in times when you look up with a heart running on empty because the world keeps on hurting you. Even only in those brief moments—you have me—a piece of home you gave away because the sky was feeling cold and empty.

I'd like to believe that we have so many lives to live together. But I guess I'm already okay with this one.

I'll take it and say it's enough.

It's impossible to take back all the pieces of myself I have given you. So please keep them safe in case I won't be there in the next life.

And if that happens...

Think of me as the little stars dancing through the night—the ones you can't see but know are there. I'll be that small twinkle of gold in every stranger's eye. It'll be your favorite color.

My sweetest downfall, for all the rest of me that is still beating,
use it not to find me or love me once again.
Instead, let it become all the love that has been deprived of you
in this and every other lifetime.

Beside yours,
the heart you painted bluest.

t y m b e r   a l d a i n e

<u>November Nightmares</u>

The night deepens

Icy fingers grip my heart

Doubts pain regret

Monsters grow tall

As whispers of winter

Starve all reason

November Nightmares

Feast on sanity

Swati Upadhyay

You Were My Wish(bone)

I remember we didn't want to break it / we *hoped that then both of our wishes would come true* / no one wins so both of us win, right? / but then we talked about your wish all night / *and I found my half of the wishbone by my bed in the morning* / then your wish came true / *and mine didn't because all I wished for was you*

C. B. Ramblings

Contributors

Abigail Alvarado

Abi Alvarado is a creative writer from Laredo, Texas, and expresses herself and her faith using the mystery of poetry. Abi has been writing poetry since she was a little girl, and poetry has often been her creative outlet. Abi takes inspiration from nature, her faith, and events in her life that only make sense when written. When Abi is not writing, she runs track and studies dietetics at Lipscomb University. Follow Abi @abi_alvarado120 on Instagram for more.

Adeola Sheehy-Adekale

Adeola Sheehy is an Irish/Nigerian Londoner now living in the New Forest, with her four home educated children. Writing from the crossroads of race, womanhood, and creativity she uses prose to tackle the questions her mind ponders most and poetry to express the feelings closest to her heart.

Adeola's debut poetry collection *Climbing In The Dark* is the honest and raw expression of the transformation we walk through after an ending as we journey from the darkness back into the light of hope and empowerment. She is a columnist for The Green Parent magazine and is the editor of The Honest Perspective publication on Medium. You can find her work at http://www.adeolasheehy/com and follow her on Instagram @adeola_moonsong

Adesiyan Oluwapelumi

Adesiyan Oluwapelumi (he/him), TPC XI, is a Nigerian writer with works published/forthcoming in BRITTLE PAPER, Kahalari Review, Lumiere Review, WRR CultureCult Press ,Literary Cocktail Magazine, Spillwords, Poemify Magazine, Beatnik Cowboy & elsewhere. His work is also featured in the Society Of Young Nigerian Writers (SYNW) 'Voices of Revolution' anthology. He writes to explore themes of boyhood & grief. He is also a chronic lover of tomatoes. Find him on Twitter @ademindpoems.

Ali Ashhar
Ali Ashhar is a poet, short story writer and columnist from Jaunpur, India. Ali Ashhar has given his thoughts a patron in the form of writing. He is an award-winning author of poetry collection, Mirror of Emotions. Apart from writing, he often loves to get lost in nature, delve in spirituality and enjoy watching his favourite football team putting up a great show.

Alina Hamid
Alina is a young Pakistani-Canadian poet, with a theatrical imagination. What was once just a few lines written in a diary once every blue moon, transcended into a strong passion for writing grandiose tales about mystical realms with faeries, queens, and haunted creatures based on real-life experiences. Alina's works embark readers on a quest to explore all the hidden meanings and revive their own sense of artistry and imagination. Her journey as a poet is only beginning, but she's delighted to have you join along and see where it may lead her. Alina's other works can be found on Instagram, @lusciousdiary.

Alshaad Kara
Alshaad Kara is a Mauritian poet who writes from his heart. His latest poems were published in one Magazine, "parABnormal Magazine September 2022;" and three anthologies, "Les gardeurs de Rêves," "Love Letters to Poe, Volume 2: Houses of Usher" and "20.35 Africa: An Anthology of Contemporary Poetry Vol. V"

Ally Bird
Ally's main subject she writes about is humanity, and she loves delving into every aspect of life. Although her humour is somewhat youthful, she has this natural ability to write from multiple perspectives in a mature yet honest manner. She writes wherever the wind takes her; be it erotic, sad, empowering, spiritual, or romantic, she loves to descend into the light and dark aspects of life. Her favourite type of writing is honest writing. She finds solace in writing as a form of escapism and sees it as spiritually therapeutic.

While poetry holds a large part of her heart, her writing doesn't stop there. At home, Ally also indulges in works of fantasy and fiction and even works that dive deep into the mental mountains of self-improvement. She's love, light, shadow work and real talk. Since 2018 she has built up a following; you can find her writing page on Facebook, Akashic Records Chapters Of Love - The Write Hand Brain.

Amal Adnan

A girl who writes when she doesn't feel alright. Writing helps her make sense of the abundance of racing thoughts that keep her up at night. When thoughts and fears are translated onto a notebook or a screen, they seem less scary and make her feel like she got this. She was a reader before she was a writer and she was a storyteller before she was a poet. But it doesn't matter if the darkness that resides within her comes out in rhymes or in prose, as long as it has somewhere to go. As a nod to her degree in psychology, her writings revolve around mental health and illnesses. She just hopes her writing would make someone feel less alone and that it's ok to not always feel ok, even when things on the surface seem fine. Now that she is entering her twenties with nothing but an overactive imagination, two loyal best friends, and herself, she is finally ready to tell her story.

Amanda Thuy

Amanda's earliest memory of writing is from the age of 8 – a poem about the color black. Since then, writing has remained a constant. From childhood to young adult, she entered writing contests, joined and attended poetry conventions. She went on to study English Literature and Law. As life and career continued, Amanda never lost her passion for writing. Her creative inspiration is drawn from many sources including love, nature, and the exploration of life's beauty and complexities. Her work explores dark and light shades of life, personal experiences as well as fantasy. Her prose/poetry has appeared in various publications over the years.

Amanda Waldron

Amanda Waldron was born in the vast Australian outback, and inherited her deep love of words from her crossword addicted mother. After a long break and many careers, she turned back to the poetry and writing she had always loved as a child to provide a creative outlet, and her works centre around themes of home, hope, family, and food. Her poetry can be found on Instagram @adoor_onceopened.

Amy Laessle-Morgan

Amy Laessle-Morgan, also known as @ultramarine_poetry, is a poet/writer who resides in Michigan. Amy's personal experience with grief/loss have helped her find writing as a means of therapy and coping. When not writing, Amy enjoys photography, music, cinema, reading and traveling. She often finds solace between the pages of books or in stacks of vinyl records. Her work has been published in the 2020 and 2021 editions of Sterling Script: A Local Author Collection. Amy was also a featured collaborative artist for the New York City concert series *Sounds Rising from Words.*

Angela Olejnik

Angela is a part-time student of English Literature and History. She enjoys metaphysical, transcendental themes and writes about beauty, hope and light in the darkness. Her poetry can be found on Instagram under the username @constellations.in.the.night.

Angelica Lyanna Nolasco Garcia

Angelica Lyanna Nolasco Garcia loved poetry ever since she took a poetry class during her senior year in high school. She enjoys writing poems with alliteration and metaphors, and she enjoys presenting her poems through spoken word. As an INFJ and an introvert, poetry gives her freedom, expression, and purpose. She is great at using pareidolia and thinking outside the box. She is honored to take part in Poetic Reveries's anthology for the first time for the theme, "Daydreams and Lost Wishes." Her poem for this particular theme is inspired by her childhood.

Ann Marie Eleazer

Ann Marie Eleazer has always considered herself a bit ancient, haunted and otherworldly, who enjoys enchanted flights through the dark fairy tales and magical places she's been drawn to since childhood. What began as a creative outlet soon became an unleashing of what lies beneath in her world of bewitching darkness and poetic passion. A lover of all things that beautifully grow in the dark, she enjoys reading, collecting antiques, and filling pages with magic while spending time with her family and fur baby.

Arya Spring

Arya Spring writes poetry as an outlet for her emotional state of being. She believes that merely recounting her thoughts, realizations, stories, and what-ifs will not depict their complexities and grandeur; emotions demand creativity.

Audrey Costa

Audrey tells pieces of her story through words and photography. She is a Health Coach and Nature Therapist by trade, but also a writer, backpacker, photographer, gourd artist and mom. She has found that writing, nature and movement have been instrumental in her healing from past traumas. She shares fragments of her story in hopes of sending the message to others that they are not alone. Find her on Instagram at @exhalingthenarrative

Avinaba Mistry

Avin is a trilingual 30 something who kept writing verses in English on and off for about a decade now. He finds his inspiration in stray feelings, unfinished conversations, and, more often than not, in a cup of coffee. Still learning more about computers in pursuit of becoming a scientist and hopes to keep writing till the end.

Berkana Vuno
Writes poetry and prose to mend her warrior spirit. She wanders between the realms of twilight and oblivion, seeking peace and serenity from all that haunts her. Beneath the veil of enigma, she bleeds ink into words, to heal her soul.

Brandi Begin
Brandi Begin is an elementary school teacher with an avid passion for writing. As someone who has struggled with mental health issues throughout her life, she finds writing to be an incredibly powerful outlet in processing the various challenges she has faced. She began sharing her poetry with a goal to inspire, motivate, and provide hope to others. Some topics she has written about include mental health, love, societal issues, and more. In her free time, she enjoys traveling with her husband, running, and spending time with loved ones. Her poems can be found on her Instagram, @BBeginPoetry.

Brittany Benko
Brittany Benko is a special needs mother, law enforcemnt wife, self-published author, Hubpages blogger, Wix poetry blogger, LitPick book reviewer, Wattpad writer, Etsy seller, and offers writing gigs on Fiverr. She lives in the Lowcountry of South Carolina.

Carla Gagen
Is a Poetess enjoying the American Midwest as she explores her roots, and follows in the steps of her ancestors exploring healing through poetry.

Carlo Fabri
Carmello Fabri is a 27 year old Lebanese emerging poet and artist with a unique style grounded in the realities of his daily life and job in psychology and social work. He is currently pursuing his master's

degree in Arts and Cultural management in France. Carmello's passion for poetry started in his early childhood years when his very first poem was published in the school's magazine at the age of 10. An Instagram account he created dedicated for his poems has been getting a lot of traction. He has been participating in poetry contests and open mics. Highlights in his poetry journey include participating in an anthology titled Ashes in the Glen as well as having one of his poems featured on a poetry website. You can check all his poems on Instagram: @fabrispoems

Cate McMinn
Cate McMinn is a poet, a dreamer, and a wannabe witch. She believes in everyday magic, laughing very loudly, and crying when necessary. She's happily married with four kids, three cats, two dogs, and a snake. Cate can be found on Instagram at @cate_mcminn.

Cathy Blue
Instagram: @thebordersofcreativity
Day-time mummy, night-time determined and bold Poetess. Cathy Blue has been writing since the age of 12 and was first drawn to poetry in her early teens, always staying true to her roots and following her own heart in her work. She has written and published 9 poetry books – 7 in English, and 2 in Turkish – and has recently taken part in the Aroma of Nature anthology by Beliterat and The Sacred Feminine Volume II: An Open Skies Collection.

Her Books: *Love Poems for A Dollar*, *Raise Your Glass To All That We've Lost*, *Loving All These Heartbreaks For Us*, *Making Love With Words*, *Fill The Cracks In My Soul With Poetry*, *Last Thoughts Before The Exit*, and *Rotten Love For Sale*.

C.B. Ramblings
C. B. Ramblings has been writing on-and-off since she was in middle school. In January of 2020, after graduating from college the month prior with both a Bachelors of Fine Art and a Bachelors of Science, she started her Instagram account @ramblingsofayoungadult to share her

poetry and help her stay creative. C.B. goes through different poetry series' to keep herself interested and creative and tends to write mostly about loss, unrequited love and heartbreak. She hopes to publish her first poetry collection in late 2023/early 2024.

C.B. also runs an online digital magazine for other people in the poetry community—Gypsophila Magazine, @gypsophilazine on Instagram.

Charlene Fox

Charlene was born and raised in a suburb south of Detroit Michigan. She started writing as a hobby in high school and stopped in her 20's when 'life got in the way'. After a long hiatus, she started hitting the computer keys in 2021 as a way of healing from her abusive past and sharing a part of her story on the website CUT19. Throughout 2022, Charlene has stepped outside her comfort zone and continued to write many forms of poetry and prose about love and relationships and has had several of her pieces published in three anthologies this year; 'Trails of Light', 'A Touch of Temptation' and 'Love is Helpless'. She also has a book of her own titled 'Acceptance' which is available worldwide on Amazon.

To read more of her writing you can find her on Facebook at facebook.com/charlenesclosetofthoughts and on Instagram at @charlenesclosetofthoughts.

Charlotte Gébert

Charlotte Gébert is a writer and poet based in Sydney. Her writing has been published in Thought Catalog, Sponge, Other Voices, Lit Up and The Creative Cafe. She completed her Bachelor of Communication at Western Sydney University. She enjoys nature walks, music, and absorbing fascinating stories. Charlotte has explored the realms of poetry and fiction writing from an early age and is eager to continue growing as a writer. For writing updates follow her on Instagram @shewrites_oceans

Chrissie Hyde

Chrissie Hyde is the poetic mirror side of Christine Yeong, former guitar teacher, performer, songwriter and anxiety coach. The Perth-based poet majored in music and marketing at the University of Western Australia. Following a relapse into severe anxiety disorder in late 2021, Chrissie turned to poetry as part of her therapeutic journey. Having found her creative spark again, she is currently seeking her debut poetry publication. Her poems are written in a rhythmic rhyming style, with a focus on emotions, nature and life.

Christine Colyer

Christine Colyer came to the art of writing as an outlet for grief after the unexpected loss of her father in 2015. Unbeknownst to her at the time, death of family members was to visit three more times in the next two years, leaving writing as her lifeline for drowning grief and despair. This writing gradually turned into sharing that turned into the gift of healing. Today she writes daily in the form of poetry, prose, and blogging on a number of topics ranging from loss in its many forms, to spirituality, to recovering from buried trauma, to the beauty and deep healing to be found in nature. She recently retired from a 40-year career spent caring for and teaching children and enjoys reading, hiking, gardening, traveling, photography, grand-parenting, and riding motorcycles -alongside her husband- as they search the country for the most scenic sweeping vistas and curvy roads to photograph as companions for her words.

Clare McKeown

Clare is a poet and illustrator from the UK who started writing to find some calm in amongst the chaos of healing from complex trauma and fibromyalgia. It is something that brings her joy and a sense of relief during those harder times – especially when it helps her to connect with others who have experienced similar things. She continually sets goals to be the person she always knew she was (before her life changed) and writing/creativity are a big part of that discovery of Self. Most, if not all, of her poems pertain to the tragedy of wishes lost, the hope for love and daydream like romance. Thus, it is the tragedy of life and the dream of everlasting love that pulls at all our heartstrings and what it means to be human – something she hopes her readers can all resonate with, therefore allowing her words to punctuate and highlight the very feelings they may not wish to admit or say out loud.

Daniel Moreschi

Daniel Moreschi is a poet from Neath, South Wales, UK. After life was turned upside down by his ongoing battle with severe M.E., he rediscovered his passion for poetry that had been dormant since his teenage years. Writing has served as a distraction from his struggles ever since. Daniel has been acclaimed by numerous poetry competitions, including those hosted by: Oliver Goldsmith Literature Festival, Wine Country Writers Festival, Ohio Poetry Day, Westmoreland Arts & Heritage Festival, Utah State Poetry Society, and Jurica-Suchy Nature Museum. Daniel has also had poetry published by The Society of Classical Poets, and The Black Cat Poetry Press.

Dawn Harrell

Dawn P. Harrell calls Southern Louisiana home where she works full-time and loves being outside. Dawn loves spending time with her 2 grown sons, her daughter-in-law, and 2 rescue dogs. A writer by hobby, she started sharing her personal writing at the encouragement of several friends, and in 2018 Dawn created a Facebook page, aptly named, Seasons of a Sewer Girl. Her writing comes from experience and much of it tends to have a darker feel to it, but that's because the words are her journey, her truth. Dawn doesn't try and hide her scars, she puts them out there for all to see. She shares her vulnerabilities and deepest thoughts to let others, who may have experienced abuse or have struggled with self-worth, know they are not alone. Dawn is shamelessly nerdy, a longtime lover of the night, and when she's not working or writing, you can find her at 3 a.m. looking at the stars and contemplating her next written piece or watching classic horror movies.

Debie Collins
Debie is an imaginative person who embraces all of life. She draws, knits, writes and paints. Her role as an educator of children with special needs gives her an outlet for her creativity. She lives in Sunny San Diego with her tortoise, 2 spaniels and husband. The outdoors is often where you will find her. She hikes, canoes and fly fishes in the Eastern Sierras and camps as often as she can. She believes that words can manifest purpose and define the power of mystery that lives in us all. Debie has a desire to share and encourage others to grow in whatever form of art helps them better understand how their life experiences are of value.

Delton John Go
Amazing, or at least Delton, Del, Delts, or DJ thinks he is. A lucky man who had the privilege of trying. Holding a bachelor's degree in Applied Mathematics, he had no real opportunity to study the arts deeply. Despite this, his artistic senses, however mediocre, called out to him. Since graduating from high school, he created a lot of doodles for him and his friends. Because of the pandemic and his boredom, this would extend to oil pastels and acrylic painting. By the end of 2021, his old love would reach out to him – poetry. He currently took on a self-challenge – to write at least one poem each week of 2022. Though some are flawed, he continues to share these poems in his Instagram page @_go.dj_. Amazing? Definitely not, but let's let Delton feel he is.

Divya Singh
Divya Singh hails from India. She writes poetic pieces based on myriad aspects of life, ranging from the philosophical to the emotional, the real to the imaginary. She loves to compose and perform spoken word poetry. Along with being a poet at heart, Divya works as an engineer in a tech firm. She writes because it helps her feel and heal and see the magic in the mundane. Hence, she often uses the pseudonym @_.magique._ to express her words.

Donna McCabe

Donna McCabe is an established poet with over twenty years experience. Her work has gained her multiple accolades within her field of literature. From being published in journals, magazines and anthologies, she is also a respected admin on social media pages as well as having her own Instagram page, @donnamccabe_ and Facebook: Poemsbydonnamccabe

Dona McCormack

Dona McCormack is a poet, writer, and mental health advocate, with fiction published in Saturday Evening Post and Tahoma Literary Review, among others, and poetry at Spillwords Press, and forthcoming at Fine Lines. She has her Masters in Arts in English and Writing Fiction. She spends her time managing her writing career and her disabilities, working her garden, and enjoying wildlife, her home, and her family. The featured piece is a selection from Dona's first poetry collection, love bytes/Love Bites, forthcoming in 2023. Connect with Dona on Instagram: www.instagram.com/itcomesdowntochance

Doug Evans

Doug and his wife Diane live near the Weber River in Oakley, Utah, USA—a pastoral mountain valley where they grew their family. Doug is a retired water and sustainability director of a large public water utility. He has served in many public positions, including on the Oakley City Council and as Mayor. Doug currently serves on the local Board of Health. He also serves as a South Summit Trails Foundation board member, believing that access to the outdoors is a lasting and effective treatment for mental health issues. As an avid hiker, biker, explorer, and naturalist, Doug has spent much of his life writing poetry and essays on water—particularly regarding the vital protection of our living lakes and rivers. He also enjoys writing about the unifying aspects of nature, science, and his strong faith. These are tonics of mercy during times of depression and anxiety as an environmental steward on the "left-hand fork of the river;" in Utah. Doug's heartfelt poetry and prose are found at: mylifeasariver.com

Dr. Vita Yo (Virahela)
Dr. Vita Yo is a medical doctor and music teacher in profession and lives in the exotic island of Bali, Indonesia. Her post-graduate degree in biomedical and music teaching majoring piano classical has gained her experience working with people with different backgrounds and age. Her heart for people allows her to reach through her words to comfort. Her love for nature and people allows her pen to write beautiful poems. Her want for growth led her to start writing in mid 2020. It has led her to create writings that touches the heart of many. She loves music and teaching it along with singing, she also enjoys reading, travelling, doing health care volunteer work and culinary. Arts of any form grabs her heart. As a mother and wife, she is a strong woman that enjoys caring for others. Her goal is to care for the human heart through her work. As she continues to use her writing to heal and inspire. IG @Virahela

Emana Mary Ann
Raye Bautista Sy is an unpublished writer from the Philippines. Writing poems and short stories became her hobbies when she won first prize during her high school English Fair.

Featured poem, LONGING was made when the author begun her fangirling journey dedicated to a guitarist who was not active in the industry. When her co-fan and close friend Vilma died due to brain surgery, this poetry became more meaningful thus dedicated to her as well.

Emily Paget
Emily R. Paget lives and works in Dumfries and Galloway, Scotland. The landscape and coast around her home inspires both her writing and photography. She often links her poetry to the photographs she takes and is passionate about her natural surroundings, history and the balance of dark and light. She shares some of her writing and photography on Instagram (@life_and_light_poetry), Facebook and Tik Tok.

She was shortlisted for the Yeovil Poetry Prize 2022 and has been published in journals and anthologies including *The Minnow Literary Magazine, First Line Poets Anthology, Hope is a Group Project, Object of My Desire* and *Daydreams & Lost Wishes*. Her debut poetry collection, *The Weight of Missing*, was published in March 2023 by The Choir Press.

Emma Hill

Emma Hill, Scottish born living in Ireland recently found poetry as a way to express feelings and make sense of experiences. After many years feeling blocked creatively she is now writing and painting. For more visit her Instagram @emmas_expressions

Raya Soleil

Raya Soleil is a woman who considers herself to be a free spirit, wandering far off the beaten path and following her wild heart in relentless pursuit of passion and an authentic life. Her writing tells the tale of her struggle to climb out of the dark abyss and back into the light—finding her truth and herself again after years of feeling broken and lost. Always a lover of words and stories, she began writing to help herself heal and to chronicle her process of becoming. Raya is so thankful to be able to share her journey on the road less traveled with other wandering souls through her words. It is her hope that her writing may serve to encourage, inspire, and/or amuse you while you travel through this life. You can find more of her original writing on her website at https://gypsysreverie.com/ or on social media at https://www.instagram.com/raya.soleil/ and https://www.facebook.com/rayasoleilwriter.

Hamna Adeel

Hamna Adeel is a nineteen-year-old girl cocooned in her own imaginary world. Vigorously scribbling her thoughts and feelings on a piece of paper. You'll often find her sipping coffee and reading a book in the corner. She hopes that her poems become a bridge connecting people's hearts with her words.

Helen C. Green

Helen C Green was born in Nottinghamshire, UK, with a passion for words and wanderlust in her heart.

Discovering a love for writing poetry in 2021, she draws inspiration from nature, a daily mindfulness practice, her healing journey from ME/CFS, and loves an evocative poetry prompt.

Living with a debilitating chronic health condition has led Helen to exploring and expressing her creativity through poetry and photography.

You can read more of Helen's poems on Instagram at @words_by_helen

Her Grey Side

Her Grey Side is an Australian Poet living and writing on the East Coast of Australia. She weaves modern poetry that comes from all the different shades of everyday living. The thoughts that are between what is black and white. Her work is inspired by nature, art and occasionally wine. She actively writes daily on Instagram, Twitter, TikTok and Facebook AND is in the process of writing her debut poetry book collection.

Isabella Quek

A girl in her 20s who always fancies a good story and decided to pick up her pen one day to write one herself and could never stop since. She loves fantasy, mystery, history and sometimes a little bit of romance would put a chuckle on her face too. To her, muse exists everywhere – the sound of bird chirping, the tale by the next-door granny, the bucket of tears thanks to the person she thought would be the one, the news on TV that connects us to people all over the world, and those countless nights where she would just stare at a blank paper and let her thoughts run wild in the small cosy room. She wants to be a poet, to put her stories into a couple of lines that connect her innermost feelings with the world. It is the simple delight that she wishes to own.

Isadora Grevan
Besides writing poetry, Isadora Grevan is an assistant professor of Brazilian and Portuguese studies at Rutgers University in the United States. She holds a BA in Comparative Literature from the University of California, Berkeley and a Masters and Ph.D. in Brazilian and Portuguese Studies from Brown University. Her first academic book is Fetishism as Structure, Image and Performance in the Theater by Nelson Rodrigues, published by Ed.UERJ (State University of Rio de Janeiro Press), December 2021.

J. Lovelace
J. Lovelace is a published writer, faith blogger, spoken word poet, and indie short filmmaker. With several years of professional and creative writing experience, J. most enjoys telling stories that illustrate the copious sides of woman in a way that echoes deeply with her readers.

J. Lovelace currently resides in Florida with her husband and two children.

Jai Michelle
Jai-Michelle is a Scottish poet, living in The Netherlands. Writing in hypnagogic, meditative states, yet rooted in her celtic culture she writes of the early loss and trauma through an imagist, mythic and natural lens. Published in various journals, her first chapbook 'A Vision of Orchid' was released in July 2022 by Sunday Mornings at the River.

Jaime Boey
Jaime Boey, who resides in Malaysia, was a technical designer for industrial packaging before becoming the operations and sales support. She started writing poetry passionately during the economic slowdown caused by the COVID pandemic. She hopes to publish her first poetry collection, titled "In the Poet's Shadow." Her poetic canvas consists of Haiku sonnets, Tanka, Sedoka, Haibun, Elfchen, Cinquain,

Monchielle, Madrigal, Ballad, Endecha, Harlequin, Septolet, Triolet, Shakespearean/Spencerian sonnets, Rondeau Redoublé, Sestina, Interlocking Rubaiyat, Ghazal, Terzanelle, Shadorma, Monotetra, Fibonacci, Strambotto, and more. Her forte is fusing expressions with techniques to create the poetic art of movement. On this note, she thanks Poetic Reveries, for the opportunity to actualize her dream of publishing poetry.

If you would like to read more of Jaime's poetry, her Instagram page is @jaimeboey.

Jay Long
Jay Long is an author, poet, entrepreneur, and founder of 300 South Media Group. He was born and raised in the awe inspiring Hudson Valley area of New York, about an hour north of NYC. Jay has 3 collections of his own writing published and works closely with indie writers and poets daily. Jay Long is an advocate for writers of all levels and experience and continues to establish himself as one of today's prolific voices of modern poetry. You can find more of his writing @WriterJayLong on both Facebook and Instagram.

JC De Ramos
Through experiencing it against their will, J has come to accept that no matter our exertions, life always finds a way of grounding us back to square one. Whether that's for better or worse, J prefers to know blindly, for now.

Jena P. August
Before writing poetry, Jena P. August received her Education degree at the University of Alberta (English/Language Arts) in 2016. Later that year, she married her husband and they had their beautiful daughter two years later. During the lockdowns of the pandemic, Jena decided to pursue her dream of becoming an author. Her first poetry collection, Sonder & Rhythm, will be available in the summer of 2023.

Jennifer Gordon
Jennifer Gordon is a poet, yoga instructor, wife and mother of three incredible children. She draws her inspiration from nature, personal struggle, deep emotion, and observations on the complexities of life. Her two books 'Poems To Read In The Rain' and 'The Nature Of Night' can both be found on Amazon and online through all major booksellers.

Jennifer Torvalson
Jennifer Torvalson is a former Rehabilitation Practitioner who has been employed in several capacities including, inner-city counsellor, personal aide and, Individual Program Plan writer for funding submissions. She has, however, woven words into prose and poetry privately, since her youth. Prompted by a transformative life event, she began to openly share her pieces, early 2022. She has since been published in the poetic anthologies: *Trails of Light, A Touch of Temptation, Memories* and *Love Is Helpless.* Although the resident Canadian is hopelessly landlocked, her writing predominantly bespeaks her ongoing love affair with the ocean and its ancient wiles. She is a pursuer of simplicity and of seeks happiness in the smallest things. When not reading or writing, she may often be found haunting second-bookstores or thrift shops and believes unwaveringly, in the beauty of imperfection. Visit her as lostlass @seaswept7 on Instagram or via Facebook.

Johannes Karlsson
Johannes Karlsson is a student of philosophy born in Sweden, 1997, and an avid reader of fantasy since 2004. After not touching (or thinking about) poetry after a short emphasis on it through school at 15, a combination between a breakup and a friend reintroduced it, and he found himself stuck. After first having his eyes opened to instapoetry, he eventually found himself in love with the romantics – as prophesised by the aforementioned friend. Stories (and beauty) is what primarily captures his mind – whether in philosophy, fantasy, or poetry. And if he could have tea with Iroh – that would all but complete his life.

Jonathan James

Jonathan E. James Jr was born and raised in the United States Virgin Islands, which is a few miles to the southeast of Puerto Rico. He's spent roughly 17 years of his adult life, living in New York City and Atlanta, Georgia, before moving back to his home of the Virgin Islands. He's been in the Instagram writing community for a little over three years and has earned a great reputation for his sharp and keen sense of word usage. He's written many, many pieces over the years and this will be his third time having one of his pieces shared by @poeticreveries_ He finds himself coming to the writing community, pretty much, every day to share his micro poems and extended pieces. Poetry has most definitely become his life calling. He considers himself to be rather blessed in his love for writing.

Jonathan Young

Jonathan Young is a poet who writes from his own experiences of life; bringing both light to the darkness and a place for his thoughts to roam freely, imaginatively and in worlds created by as he describes it, his own elaborated truth.

J. Sexton

J. Sexton lives in the north-west of England with her son and two cats. She began writing at a very early age as a way of expressing her creativity, but only found the courage to allow others to read her work in 2012. Nowadays, she shares her work regularly on Facebook, Instagram, and Wattpad, and is currently working on a novel set in the medieval period.

She is a lover of nature, history, paganism and the supernatural, silly humour, and red wine. In her spare time, when she isn't writing, she enjoys naps, watches horror movies and serial killer documentaries, and listens to classic rock. She is partial to a mini Guinness.

J. Sexton has published three poetry books, *Her Undisclosed Desires*, *Small Stories*, and *Ghosts*, and you can find her on Instagram at @fragmentspoetry and @herundiscloseddesires, and on Facebook at

@fragmentsofmymind. She is the founder and editor-in-chief of Poetic Reveries.

Julia Sophia Brown
Julia Sophia Brown is a neurodivergent writer and poet. Julia writes Poetry across all genres with a special interest in dark and shadowy topics. @poetryfromsophia

Julia Yee
Julia Yee is a poet at heart and a dreamer in her soul. She recently moved from New York City to Paris, and when she is not daydreaming while walking along the Seine, she posts original poetry on her Instagram page (day.dream.diaries), writes children's books, freelance copy-writes, and co-hosts a book themed podcast (Meet Me At The Bookstore).

Kairos Moira
Kairos was born in the UK, he began writing as a way to try and interpret not only the world that surrounds him, but also his inner thoughts and feelings. Creating imagery within the metaphorical became a visual tool for interpretation. His entire body of work originates from personal emotions and experience. His work may often seem abstract, or simple. However, if you look beyond the written, you will simply find a man who is trying to understand the world in which he lives.

Karen Chan
Born in Hong Kong, Karen, a sixteen-year-old poet, has been passionate about poetry since the age of five. She bleeds on paper and loiters in a labyrinth of chimeras.

Words haunted by the inundation of midnights and entrapment of her aching thoughts, she seeks solace by exploiting her shattered pieces to craft spells, and she calls them poetry.

She dreams of people all around the world, loving in the language of poetry.

Her poems can be savored in her Instagram account @hxpelessr

Karthik Raichurkar
He is a doctor, a transplant surgeon, with a part time interest in writing. He lives in Bengaluru, India and keen on sharing life experiences through his writings.

Karuna Mistry
Following the death of his mother, Karuna Mistry suddenly woke up to poetry (literally). He is a British writer of Indian ethnicity. Over the past year, he has had his poetry published in various anthologies including McKinley Publishing Hub, Open Door, and Sweetycat Press. His creative writing interests are thoughtful and broad; covering biology, nature, science fiction and spirituality. Karuna is currently working on his debut release. Instagram: @karunamistrypoetry

Katherine Cota MacDonald
Katherine Cota MacDonald, kat.herinecm, was born and raised in Massachusetts. A writer at heart, she began writing poetry in her youth and has ushered life's transitions into her pieces. Threads of nature, grief, parenting, joy, solitude, and the tide of the creative spirit most prominently line the pockets of her works. Katherine is an artist, educator, and wellness advocate and she is currently pursuing her MSW.

Kathryn Holeton
Kathryn Holeton is a poet, author, and native Tennessean. Kathryn's poetry has recently been published in *The Plum Tree Tavern*, *The Academy of the Heart and Mind*, and the *Dreams in Hiding Anthology*,

among others. She enjoys listening to music and reading in her free time.

K.R. Wieland

K.R. Wieland has always had an over-abundant love of creating, whether it is with paintbrush, pen, or typing away at her computer. When she is not writing or painting, you can find her at home dancing in the kitchen with her daughters or talking all things nerdy or foodie with her husband. You can read more of her poetry in Crow Calls: Vol 1-5, and her own collection, Battlefield Heart.

Kelly Riddle

Kelly Riddle is a twenty-one-year-old author and poet. Her first book 'Noise' was published in 2019. She is currently an undergraduate behavioral neuroscience and philosophy student at Northeastern University in Boston. She has many plans for future books. Her Instagram, Facebook, and TikTok handles are all @kellyyriddle.

Kelsey Singh

This will be Kelsey's first submission of the like. She was born in North Carolina but has now made a home in Virginia, Maryland, and now Fairfield, California with her husband Spencer, a rescue kitty named Kenneth, and two rescue dogs — a weenie named Moxxi and a hound named Lernie.

She enjoys creating and sprinkling her corner-nook desk (Ethel), house, as well as family and friends with random assortments of poetic parchments from her 1970's avocado manual typewriter (Patrick). These pieces usually range from whimsical, spicy, and eccentric to deeply personal, private, and emotional. She attempts to explore all of the surreal ways that our experiences with existence can be deliberately spoken into a timeless life of their own and hopes to stir the minds and hearts of anyone that may stop by and read her work.

Kerryanne Brown

Kerryanne is a keen writer and scientist based in Liverpool, United Kingdom. Science is the love of her mind; poetry is the love of her heart. Kerryanne started writing as an outlet and completely fell in love with poetry. She has recently released her debut book "Imperfect Poems from an Imperfect Mind," which explores the changeability of the mind. Kerryanne takes inspiration from love, nature and life's varying moments, challenging herself to improve her poetry every day. She hopes some of her work can help to inspire you! You can find more of her work at @kayabeecollection on Instagram.

Kiera Gold

Kiera Gold is a novelist and poet with a Master's degree in creative writing from Bridgewater State University. Ms. Gold enjoys playing with mythological, magical, and natural themes in her pieces, and loves exploring the outside world with her pup, Daisy. She has been previously published in "Otherworldly Women Magazine" and hopes to connect with others through the gift of writing. You can find more of her poetry on Instagram @golden_pressed

Kimberley Sasha Coutinho

She is a Physiotherapist by profession and a writer by passion. She started writing to express herself in ways she thought she couldn't open up to people. She first began expressing herself and her emotions in her Diary, and gradually decided to start writing for the world to read. Writing made her realize that she could reach out to people through her words and make them realize, that they were not alone. Writing has helped her overcome her anxiety and has also helped her realize that she is better than what she thought she was. Being a poet has been the best thing that has happened to her in a while.

Krissie Wolf

K.Wolf, aka Krissie, lives in a small town in Ontario, Canada. She started writing as a way of healing her heart from unfortunate events of life. Finding love and fulfillment in writing, Krissie now lives a life filled of love and gratitude.

Kristin Carroll
K.G. Carroll is a poet residing in Central Valley California. She grew up roaming the orange fields and vast golden hills that rest beneath the magnificent Sequoia National Forest. Alone with herself and her thoughts only as company, finding an escape from the harsh realities of home, she found a love for words. Rhyming, word play, and her vivid imagination faced no boundaries. Surviving repeated emotional turmoil and upheavals she found herself in while growing up, discovering adulthood, and escaping generational patterns of abuse, her words, though tainted with darkness are etched with bravery and resilience. It's with these words she hopes to touch her readers leaving behind a glimmer of hope in a world often painted black.

Lakshyaa Velmurugan
is an amateur writer who is documenting her thoughts by channelizing them into short poems.

Laura Lewis
Laura Lewis is a woman filled with an undying devotion to her own becoming and the mother of three beautifully wild children. During this fleeting season of her life, she is searching for the muse in every stolen moment. For as long as she can remember writing has been the way she has woven her own meaning into the world. It is through this work that her formerly starved soul has grown satiated once again. it is her fondest wish that her words might offer some sustenance to those women who are still hungry and howling for more.

Lauren Lee Verse
Lauren Lee Verse is from Pittsburgh, PA. She is a linguaphile and logophile. She is a French teacher, and an aspiring indie author in speculative fiction, working on her first novel. She has been writing for most of her life, and now she would like to start doing it full-time. She holds an M.A. in French Language and Literature, and did two years of

coursework towards a PhD, but never finished. When she's not writing, she can be found watching nerdy tv shows and movies, reading, crocheting, and playing personal chauffeur to her 7-year-old son. She also has a passion for travel and has a side gig as a travel agent. She has a very sassy cat named Luna who likes to walk across her keyboard for fun.

Lindsay Peckham
Lindsay Peckham is a mixed media artist and poet. Her artwork and writing are inspired by everyday simplicities, travel, love, and nature. She resides in Massachusetts with her daughter Lyla. Her favorite place to travel is the island of Terceira in the Azores. Often the inspiration of her works.

Instagram: @lindsaypeckhamart
Facebook: facebook.com/lindsaypeckhamart

Maggie Watson
Maggie Watson was born in Cape Town, South Africa. She now lives in the quiet seaside town of Musselburgh, Scotland. Her poetry journey began in 2020 at the start of the Pandemic and she has since, self-published three collections of poetry. Her writing draws on every aspect of life, and her own experiences. Her writing can sometimes be raw, bur Maggie feels that makes it more relatable and always hopes that one poem will resonate. For more examples of her work, you can visit her Facebook, Instagram or YouTube Channel.
https://www.facebook.com/sweetangelbutterfly
https://www.instagram.com/intheshadowofthepen/
https://www.youtube.com/channel/UCY-yZJI16OQR4_GnbZD7SqA

Maggie has CFS (chronic Fatigue Syndrome). When she is not writing she volunteers for Barnardo's.

Marc Francesc
Marc Francesc is a Catalan and Spanish LGBTQ+ amateur writer who was born in 1994 and lives in Barcelona. Some of the creative resources

409

used by the author are the reiteration of images throughout the texts with a touch of dirt, mystery and often fierce energy. His texts are always written with the intention of taking the reader on a beautiful journey through vivid imagery, you can find them on Instagram @sailorletters

Maria Hayward
Maria Hayward is an English poet, living in London. She discovered her passion for writing at a later stage in her life. Her poetry focuses on many topics including relationships, healing, growth and mental health. Maria is a keen nature lover (especially, her favourite willow trees), and her poetry is often enthused with elements of nature imagery. Over the last year, or so, Maria has developed a strong Instagram following on her poetry page @mlhmusings.

Maria has studied both Psychology and mental health at college and university, and has worked in the charity sector since 2010, in a variety of roles. Maria has a strong understanding and compassion for the human condition. She hopes, by sharing her own experiences through her poetry, she can support others to overcome, and possibly grow from, their emotional wounds.

Marx K
Growing up as a single kid, Marx's friend circle was mostly occupied by books. Books gave him company in his solitude. He grew up reading myths, fantasies and dreamed of a similar world. Being an introvert, it was difficult for him to communicate via speech. Words came to his rescue and he found it easier to talk through his words. Thus, he turned to writing down his thoughts and instincts rather than speaking them out.

MeadowZ
MeadowZ is a writer from Ho Chi Minh city, Vietnam. She loves reading, writing and taking photos whenever she can manage during her journeys. Always a storyteller, MeadowZ hopes to see more of the world, learns new things, meets amazing people and works harder for

the voices of women and people who are struggling to find their ways in life. Her motto is "Your true values lie in your stories, experiences and memories."

Meenakshi Malhotra
She is not fixed to any particular genre of poetry. She looks beyond the horizon and tries to portray everything through her poetry.

Meg Judge
Meg Judge is a writer and poet based in the Pacific Northwest. She draws inspiration from both her inner and outer life, often using her writing to unpack the deep truths of her past, present and future through a lens of self-compassion and love. Her hope is that in sending her work into the world, it will resonate with the hearts of kindred souls, foster awareness and perpetuate beauty. You can find more of her work on Instagram @_goodness.gracious_ or contact her at megjudgewrites@gmail.com to find out about upcoming showings and projects.

Meg Dring
Meg, known as msdpoetry on Instagram, began writing poetry when she was in her teens, with her work gaining structure relatively recently through increased support from friends. Being a Gemini, her work is mainly ruled by her emotions, and this is acutely evident in most of her work, there are hints of love, depression, and despair in many of her pieces which are worded with understated eloquence. She is working on two collections currently; her primary being constructed around the concept of her Ribcage and a city that resides within her chest. The focus of this collection is on people she once held dear but have left such an impact on her that they have erected houses in her chest, along the streets which are her ribs, to remain there forevermore. Her work is worth a read if you want something fresh and exciting, that occasionally sledgehammer's you in the feelings with how beautifully it is penned and the imagery she creates within her words.

Meha Khan

Meha, born 2001, is a writer and artist. She loves writing poetry, which is often inspired by her passion of painting, that brings to life, precious moments on blank pages. She aims to evoke positive emotions and reflections through her words and works alike.

Melanie Simangan

Melanie Simangan is an aspiring writer from Los Angeles, CA. She obtained her BA from UCLA and MBA from Pepperdine University. By day she writes grants for local nonprofits; by night she writes creatively on love, loss, and addiction through her Instagram, @sonnetandahalf.

Melissa Nickert

A secret writer for many years, Melissa often describes herself as a "closet writer." After the pain of divorce and the deaths of her father and brother, (only nine months apart in 2020), Melissa gathered the courage to share her musings through her words. The journey of reinventing oneself and sharing hope and even joy on the other side of pain has become her passion. Her strong faith and warrior spirit is evident in all she does and writes. When she is not writing, she can be found working as an award winning Interior Designer and mucking out the stalls of her beloved horses that she shares acreage with outside of hometown Cincinnati, Ohio. Melissa also lived 27 years in Los Angeles, CA and while there was a noted actress and producer of theater as well as a Montessori School teacher. Her BA in Design is from Miami University, Oxford Ohio. Her MA in Education and Psychology is from Pepperdine University, Malibu CA. You can find her on Instagram at @warriorofspirit.

Michael Bruan

Michael Bruan is a father, husband, teacher, and sometimes, poet. An English teacher with almost 20 years of experience across three unique schools, Michael has had the good fortune to share his love of literature and fundamental nature of inquiry with his students. Still, it is his family that matters to him most—for those are the relationships that live in his poetry. He is the author of a collection of poems called "Spiritus", a book which explores the complexity of the human condition in six distinct thematically arranged sections. Capable of distilling both pithy observations and complex poetic narratives, Michael Bruan is a poet in command of his craft.

Mohammad Allouch

Mohamad Allouch is a Lebanese writer. He develops himself in prose and poetry about love, loss, romance and intimacy. He aims in his writing to break the stigma around sexuality and to provide representation of queerness in his middle eastern environment. Being a bit of a lone wolf, he writes, edits and publishes on his own; a fact that makes this paragraph an autobiography that he managed to put down after a million attempts because he is loath to discuss himself in the third person.

With that being said, it is safe to claim that he, in spite of him speaking like he ate a dictionary for breakfast, is an idiosyncratic young adult that loves to dance and to read romcoms. He also is on Instagram as mohamad allouch.

Monique Hemingway

Monique Hemingway is an author, psychic-medium, channel and healer. In addition to her work as a prolific medium, she's also an accomplished writer and poetess. Her personal story of spiritual awakening, "Alone" was published in the book "Warrior Women with Angel Wings" (2017). Her love of poetry has been lifelong. Her words capture the gamut of human emotions and experiences and have a way of really hitting "home" with all who engage with them. Monique's favorite works are her erotic poetry collection, focusing on eroticism and poetic words as a means to help men and women integrate the sacred aspects of their sexuality as a means to heal their mind, body, and soul. Monique can be reached at: www.moniquehemingway.com Instagram: @monique_hemingway

413

Najaree Ratanajiajaroen
She's based in Bangkok, Thailand; but otherwise has been to many places, yet everywhere.

Would like to be many things but many things are too confusing. Conjugation and conjectures are what she loves; including pets and sweet things. Instagram: @labyelow

Navina Baur
Navina Donata Baur was born and raised in Germany and is currently living on the Mediterranean island of Mallorca.
Books have always been a welcome refuge for her. Growing up, she was very shy, and her introverted soul loved to sit on her bed, getting lost on foreign worlds and forget about the noisy world around her. At some point, she started to write, and found she was better at expressing her feelings and sharing her thoughts on paper. It is probably no surprise she decided to study literature and cultural studies later. Besides writing poetry, another passion, and refuge, of hers is music. When she is not writing, or reading, you can find her playing the violin. If you like to read more of her poetry, and see what she is up to, you can find her on Instagram @onedonata or visit her
website www.onedonata.com

Nicole Carlyon
A sensitive soul, day dreamer, dabbling in random words as a form of escape from a past that eludes her. Nicole writes to help heal, in the hope that in doing so she can touch others and make them feel less alone in a world that doesn't always make sense. Raw and real, the words that flow come from her soul and she does not apologise for being herself (although she is still on a journey to find out who she is).

Nikitha Senny

Nikitha Senny is an 18-year-old aspiring writer and budding poet. Born and brought up in India, her academic interests lie in the field of Architecture and she is presently awaiting university acceptance.

Currently, she posts poems on her Instagram page @random_shades_of_pastel. She is grateful to have her poems as a medium of expression and also for the time spent creating them over the past 3 years. In her free time, she loves to journal, sketch and learn new things.

Oksana Maskulka

Oksana Maskulka is a writer and poet from Toronto, Canada. Her work focuses on the depth and complexity of emotion as well as the intersection between mental health and spirituality. Read more of her work on Instagram by following @heartlessnarrator.

Olivia Bella

Olivia Bella is a poet, writer, and author of *Spicy Dreams & Sugary Lies*. Her poetry has inspired pianist, Margin Alexander, to compose a piece and perform it during one of his concerts in New York City. She's known for her sensual and elegant writing style which is largely influenced by her own life experiences as well as her love for story-telling, visual arts and music. She often writes about love and relationships with raw emotional poignancy. Olivia was born and raised in Hungary, however, she has been living and working abroad for many years, mainly in Europe as well as briefly in the United States.

Parul Shanker

Parul Shanker, aka P.S., grew up in the beautiful quiet town of Obra, Uttar Pradesh. Growing up, she was fascinated with music, nature, and books and spent most of her time in the school library, running away from Mathematics. This led to some early exposure to reading & later a passion for storytelling. Parul has won various music & art competitions, been an NCC cadet, a Sales Professional, and a Travel Enthusiast and is currently exploring Digital Content Creation on her

IG: travelwithmestranger. Parul writes in the wee morning hours; then spends the rest of the day trying to impress her online followers and planning for the next nap.

Prachi Singh
We all have broken pieces of ourselves which we shy away from sharing with people. Having experienced similar things and desired to look at the world differently, she aspires to speak for all those people who haven't voiced their feelings and emotions and help them heal through her words. In her free time, you can find her reading, exploring a new place or doodling!

Precious Magdaleno
Precious Magdaleno was born in the Philippines and raised there. She is a wedding planner, an aspiring writer, an artist, and a freelance event stylist. Precious values her faith and family the most and draws inspiration from them in her daily life. She began writing in 2015, after falling in love with literature and the arts. She finds it therapeutic to write about anything that inspires her. She'll either write something worth reading or do something worth writing about. You can connect and follow her on Instagram: @jeam.precieux

Priti Tiwari
Priti Tiwari, a teacher by profession and a writer by passion who believes that reading and writing makes us better human beings. To appreciate good writing brings her immense joy. She is an Indian immigrant residing in the USA with her husband and children. She is working towards publishing her debut poetry collection. She likes to play with words as much as with her children and suffers from tepidophobia!

RS
RS is a denizen of Delhi, India who writes Poetry to find harmony in life. She had fallen in love with versing during her days as a student of

literature. She rises early to feel inspired with the morning star and create new rhymes.

Raye Bautista Sy
Raye Bautista Sy is an unpublished writer from the Philippines. Writing poems and short stories became her hobbies when she won first prize during her high school English Fair.

Priyasha Panda
The poetess is an MD in Community Medicine and she also aspires to be a Writer. She hails from a small town, Bhawanipatna, in Kalahandi district of Odisha,India.She finds home in the beauty of nature. A logophile who weaves words in her passion for writing poetry which she posts in her Instagram handle @whirlpool_of_hearts. A daydreamer who imbibes plenty of hope from the magic of vast sky.

R. Deshea Poetry
Rebecca lives with her husband and children in a little Appalachian town where she spends a lot of her free time dreaming up curiosities to write about. She loves being outdoors and is often visually inspired by things she sees while enjoying the beauty of her surroundings. She is currently working on her master's degree for Clinical Counseling, and though she loves time alone, she also enjoys the puzzle of unraveling the mystery of thought and choices in the people she works with. She enjoys collecting feathers and rocks, old relics or rarities and finding wildflowers to press. She dreams to one day release her own book of prose inspired by life experiences and colourful imagination.

Rekha Balachandran
Rekha Balachandran is a freelance editor and author. Poetry by author Edgar Allan Poe and Classics by William Shakespeare and Louisa May Alcott are a great inspiration for her to write. Her recently published poetry books are She Wears Scars Like Constellations and

Off the Beaten Track. When she is not writing, she loves painting. She goes by @rekhasjournal on Instagram.

Renée Novosel

Renée Novosel is a writer, lover of poetry, and lifelong student of philosophy, religion, and spirituality. She was introduced to poetry as a child through the whimsically profound writing of Shel Silverstein and has early memories of experimenting with creative writing. Renée has been featured in several poetry publications and blogs, including *Poet's Garden Alchemist*, *The Auctores Monthly*, and *Authority Magazine*. *Life as an Onion*, Renée's debut poetry collection, explores life's caustic sting and transformative potential for decadence, following a timeline of heartbreak, exploration, spirituality, and healing. Renée lives in the rolling hills of Pittsburgh, US, with her children, loving partner, fauna, and flora.

Reon Sylvester D Cunha

A Chemist by profession and a writer by passion. He is from Mangalore, India. He started writing during the lockdown time. Since then, he has written many poems and short stories which are published in various anthologies and featured by many Instagram pages. He loves to pen down random thoughts during free time. Learning something new every day is his passion. Other than that, he is fond of collecting coins commemorating various events. He posts his writings on Instagram @world_of_.stories

Rozalyn Walton

Rozalyn Walton is an aspiring poet and writer from Kannapolis, North Carolina. When she was younger, you could always find her with her nose in a book. Now, she fills up her free time making stories of her own. She loves her family, friends, and her many crafty hobbies, and she always writes with that love in mind. She typically posts her writings under the alias @rozalynwrites on Instagram, but she dreams of her name filling up bookshelves one day. This anthology is the first publication of her work.

R.Z.O'Connor

R.Z.O'Connor usually known as R is a poet currently based in Istanbul, Turkey. She is a 28 years young woman who has experienced death from up close. She was introduced to poetry after surviving a traumatic incident and one day, while writing a random journal entry, she wrote her very first poem, and from then onwards, began her journey as a Poet. She writes about mental health, depression, love, tragedies, and a lot more based on her own life experiences and her observations of the world. She is publishing some exclusive and on-demand poetry on her Patreon for now and her first poetry book is in work and will be published by the end of this year on Amazon.

Reach her out on her social media: Instagram: @rzufuk
Twitter: @intotherambles_

S.A. Quinox

S.A. Quinox is a writer of silent ache. Quinox is currently 25 years old and resides in Belgium. She is a poet that writes from the abyss and resurfaces with a loving melancholy from its depths. She bleeds for those among us in search of healing. She has authored two books, 'Tales of Lacrimosa' and 'Immortalis', and can be found on social media under her pen name.

Saba Ahmed

Sabah Ahmed is a published author and a nomad of human nature, scribbling her detached thoughts with the aid of poetry and prose while hiding with good conscience behind the penname Abierto Reino. A mixture of all things desi and not, she searches for words that birth the many facets of what makes us human in the end. The edges and the dark crooks of the human soul are a big part of what her poetry originally was meant to investigate, though there is a good spot for love and hope as well. Great believer of chocolate solves everything, and fresh brewed latte should be public property, she caffeinates her way through life. Her book 'Shapes of Water' was published on Amazon in 2020 and she is currently querying her first middle grade book. You can find more of her dabbles and scribbles on her profile @abiertoreino. This piece is a remembrance of her dream of travelling the world when she was young and still believed in unconditional love.

Saiqah Salim
Saiqah Salim lives in the United Kingdom with her four inspirational children wrapped in madness. Saiqah is a Forensic Psychology graduate and works in mental health. Saiqah has been writing since 1997 and has a published piece in The Redbeck Anthology of British South Asian Poetry edited by Debjani Chatterjee, she writes to give emotions and life experiences a closure and hopes her words have a positive impact on those that read them.

Samantha Marsters
Samantha Marsters is an amateur poet/prose writer from New Zealand. Using the pseudonym JustSammy, Samantha uses a mix of both critical and creative thinking approaches to her writing. Samantha bases most of her musings on her own experiences and learning, occasionally finding inspiration in nature, the worldly and the divine. Samantha contributes her writing to her pseudonym Instagram page with one contribution to her first anthology 'Untangled' Allegories of the Mind. Still developing her craft Samantha seeks to complete her own book and share her musings and experiences with the world.

Sammy T. Anderson
Sammy T. Anderson was born and raised in small town Pierceton, Indiana, where he dreamed of becoming a writer and filmmaker. He spent most of his early adulthood traveling the United States and working in the independent film industry. Although he has written his whole life, he has only recently started pursuing publishing, with his first published piece being featured in the online magazine "Halcyon Days". He currently resides in North Hollywood, California with his wife and three dogs.

Seth Duval
Seth Duval is a poet born and raised in Philadelphia, PA. He is a Case Manager by day and a poet by night. He has been published in *Unchaining Freedoms*, a trilogy published by Ink Gladiators Press.

shamik banerjee
shamik banerjee is a poet and poetry reviewer from the North-Eastern belt of India. He loves taking long strolls and spending time with his family. His deep affection with solitude meddles well with peace and Poetry provides him an ageless harbourage of happiness. He has recently founded a poetry journal and aims to contribute immensely towards its future.

Shanmugaa Bharathi S R
Shanmugaa Bharathi S R is an aspirant writer and has published some of her works in several anthologies. She wishes to become a prolific writer one day. She started writing from eighth grade and has actively been writing since then. She aims to bring to the public the emotions and expressions of the mind and heart through her writing. She posts her work on social media under the name, The Silent Stanzas (@the_silent_stanzas).

Shaye Wallace
Shaye Wallace a poet from Southern NSW best known for her intricately worded cosmic poetry style encompassing the vast struggles of mental health and heart ache. She hopes to locate all of the wounded souls and guide them to a home of understanding.

Shelley Sanders-Gregg
Shelley Sanders-Gregg (she/her) is a writer, poet, and quote creator from St. Louis, Missouri. She is a happily married mother of four amazing kids. She holds a master's degree in social work and is a former licensed clinical social worker and therapist. She became chronically ill eleven years ago and, although she has dabbled in writing since her

teens, she started writing more frequently at that point. She found that it not only helped her release her own emotions, but her words could also be a source of healing and support to others. Other than writing, her hobbies include: swimming, traveling, herbalism, all forms of art, and watching sunsets. You can find more of her work on IG: @sgreggwrites. Shelley has been published in several anthologies including: *Descendants of Medusa, And I Healed, Dreams in Hiding,* and *Not Ghosts, But Spirits II.*

Shreya S Bharadwaj

A literature enthusiast young adult, Shreya S Bharadwaj believes that not only is a pen mightier than the sword, but is also mightier than medicines, for they can heal you on the inside, without any complications or side effects. She gives a character to each voice in her head and lets them drive her imagination and creativity. Nature is her biggest muse and she writes about life, love, chaos and melancholy by drawing a truce.

She houses the words that wander in her thoughts, by writing their fates into various literary pieces. Her biggest aspiration is to be a refuge to her readers, the very way she finds a sanctuary on her worldly itinerary. Thus, she calls her account Ritsya_haven. Join her as she gives you a tour around the castle of her mind!

She goes by @ritsya_haven on Instagram, MAKTUB - 'the fate I write' - on Twitter and has a blog site for her literary pieces of various genres - https://maktubiwrite.wordpress.com

Sirin Jezkova

Shireen, or Sirin Jezkova by full name, is a writer of mixed European and Caucasian origins. Born in 1991, currently moving between different places. Her true home is in the mountains, preferably the mountains of Armenia.

Siya Sawhney
Siya Sawhney is an aspiring young writer with a strong passion for poetry, literature, and reading. Writing is a way that she can express herself, channel her emotions, and organize her thoughts. It also enables her to explore her inner self and better understand the world around her through keen observations of things like nature. She has written two poetry collections, Catharsis and Home, both of which can be found at her Instagram handle @homeforpoetry. She truly hopes her writing can resonate with her audience and inspire budding poets to express themselves.

Sneha Sagare
Sneha Sagare is an 18-year-old writer from India. She is a student and aspires to be a surgeon and follows writing as a passion. Her writings express emotions and feelings mostly through storytelling. The vast imaginary world in her head is organised in meaningful words and rhymes. She firmly believes that words may or may not change the world but can surely inspire you to start. You will mostly find her engrossed in a book or daydreaming about a whole new world. She hopes to write as much as she could, to improve as she grows and to make many know that they are not alone in life's turmoil. Along with writing she also loves dancing, painting and trying new things. Her goal in life is to complete her long bucket list and share the emotions, stories, difficulties and people she met achieving it through her writings. You can contact her on Instagram at _snehasagare.

Sonal Bains
Sonal Bains was born in Punjab and raised in Pilibhit, a beautiful city located at the foothills of Shivalik range sharing a border with Nepal. She started writing poems as soon as she could form a sentence. Her earliest work would make its way to school display boards. Sonal is electronics engineer by education and a Patent Analyst by profession. She is also a student of law. When she is not juggling between her work, studies, and being a mum to her precious two-year old daughter, she enjoys nature walks and working on her poetry. Sonal publishes poetry on social media regularly and is currently working on her first book. You can follow Sonal's latest work on Instagram @thatquietgirl2022.

Stephanie Haveman
Stephanie Haveman, also known as AmL is a 35-year-old mother, writer, and recovering addict who has gained popularity among poets and writers. Her debut poetry collection titled "Butterflies and Guitars" touches upon topics such as love, heartbreak, family dynamics, depression, trauma, and addiction recovery. Despite facing numerous challenges in life, AmL has turned towards writing to express herself creatively. While she may be introverted in public, her pen speaks volumes on paper.

Stuti Sinha
Stuti is an Indian writer & musician, who lives in Dubai, UAE. She writes primarily about the human experience and emotions. Being passionate about travel, she loves to weave different cultures and her heritage into her writing. In 2022, she won the International Westmoreland Award for short fiction & The International Allingham Festival Prize for Poetry. She also received an honourable mention in the International Globe Soup Short Memoir Contest, and was long-listed for the International Erbacce & International Gloucestershire Poetry Contests. She previously has an honourable mention in the 2021 Annual Haiku Competition by *The Society of Classical Poets* and has been published by them, by *Sky Island Journal, Celestite Poetry, Moss Puppy Magazine, Slice of Life Lit Mag, Duck Duck Mongoose Mag*, and *Sonder Magazine*. She has also been published in the *Unchaining Freedom Anthology Trilogy* by Ink Gladiators Press (2022) and *First Line Poets Anthology* (2022). Stuti is an animal lover and has a fur baby whose name is Yuki.

Swati Upadhyay
Swati Upadhyay resides near Delhi, India. She loves to read, write and crochet. She strives to find beauty in tiny moments of live. Writing poetry for her is a way of expressing her feelings and help her make sense of this chaotic world. She hopes her words resonate with her readers and bring solace.

T.B. Elden

T. B. Elden is a new writer to the poetry scene, beginning her journey in April of 2022. Writing found her after diving deep into her mental recovery, allowing her words to finally flow. She is a proud wife and stay-at-home mother to a beautiful two-year-old girl, in Winnipeg, MB, Canada. She loves to spend time with her family, enjoying the outdoors – whether it's a morning walk or a fun camping trip. She hopes to publish a book of some of her works in the next coming year, which will include topics around trauma and healing. Her ultimate goal is to help break the stigma surrounding Borderline Personality Disorder, and to help others realize they're not alone.

Tammy Muehlfelder

Tammy is a dreamer; creative, imaginative, and a lover of life's magic. She is an introvert and an empath, who lives her life with strong emotions that are reflected in her writing style. The free flow of words, how they weave together so elegantly and intensely, and how they inspire others, has always been a fascination to her. Tammy writes because poetry calls to her heart and beckons her soul. She writes because she believes words can show others the beauty of the world as seen through her eyes. A lot of Tammy's poetry embraces romance and nostalgia while incorporating nature and moments captured in still time through her photography. She adores recording sunrises, chasing sunsets, and pairing both with her words. Her writings and photography can be found in her debut book of poetry, Endeavors of Love, available on Amazon and on Instagram @thebohemianreview

Tayane de Oliveira

Tayane de Oliveira from Germany has been writing since she was 13 years old. Now at 27 years of age, she writes poetry, short histories and music. Her work is often dark and melancholic, but at times when the inspiration comes, romantic as well. Tayane's writing is very personal and sensitive. For this reason, she hasn't shared her work often. This Anthology is a big step for her self growth and acceptance in the writers' Community.

Tejasvee Nagar

Tejasvee Nagar are an avid reader. Their pronouns are he/she/they. They follow literary news and keep themselves updated about the literary world as they plan to pursue their degree in English. They have a keen interest in poetry, cooking, baking as well as creating playlists for leisure.

Tessa Glasgow

Tessa Glasgow is a poetess from the mid-western United States. She primarily shares her work on Instagram under the username @deadofnightpoetry. Tessa self-published her debut poetry collection, "Wildfire From Hell: Poetry and Prose" on August 11th, 2021. Tessa's goal when writing poetry is to pen emotions and experiences based in reality that readers can actually relate to. She tends to use ominous and vividly eerie imagery through dark metaphors to make her pieces come to life. She uses poetry to process past traumas, chronic pain, mental struggles, and the raw human experience.

Tiffany O'Brien

Tiffany began writing poetry at the age of 14 and loved it so much she attempted a degree in Creative Writing. As fate would have it, she ended up with a degree in English Literature and History, which looks great on the wall. Tiffany enjoys music, art and the written word. For the past 24 years, she has written whenever the muse has come calling. She currently resides on the east coast of Australia with her two sons.

tymberaldaine

The sound that falls in the forest and echoes amongst flowers. Timberrr! A Surrealist Artist and Poet.

Twinkle Jain

Twinkle Jain is a 26-year-old budding writer from Jaipur, Rajasthan, India. She is a postgraduate with a Masters in Computer Application from the University of Rajasthan.

Writing came to her as a hobby, a way to share her imagination and perspective toward things around her.

A creative personality by heart, she has a deep liking for acting, singing, painting, and traveling apart from writing her heart out. She has been an active participant in several writing contests organized by the IG writing communities and has achieved accolades for the same. She has also been a co-author for a few anthologies.

Umme Huzayfah

Umme Huzayfah is a self published poet with her love of writing going back to her early years in secondary school, where encouraged by her teacher she used poetry as a form of expression of her feelings. She often uses poetry as a way to reflect, reform and realign. She writes on various topics such as self love, hope, self discovery showcasing her work on her Instagram platform @alqalampoetry . She has till now published four books with her debut book, The Flower Bloomed, available on Amazon.

Valerie Leyden-Morffi

Valerie is a full-time working, single mother (now married), raising her son in downstate New York, in the foothills of the Catskill Mountains. She is a passionate soul, with a zest for life, who loves and feels things in a big way, highly attuned and sensitive to her surroundings. Valerie developed an affinity for the written word at an early age. As an adolescent, writing became a catharsis. Restless, and a bit rebellious, Valerie finished high school early, graduating with her A.A. in Liberal Arts, at 18. In 2005, she earned her B.A. in Psychology, graduating Magna Cum Laude.

Other passions include cooking, photography, traveling the world, being a mother, singing in the car, Irish coffee, and enjoying a good whiskey and cigar night! Valerie is a lover of the creative arts… all her writings are raw and real, coming from life experience and the depths of her soul.

You can find more of Valerie's work on Facebook, Instagram, and her Website, which is still a work in progress at this time. Valerie has also been published in both the Rise from Within, Trails of Light, and A Touch of Temptation anthologies by Jay Long (300 South Media Group) and Broken Hearts – Healing Words by A.B. Baird Publishing where one of her poems, "Light as a Feather," won the People's Choice award.

Vandana Pamulaparthy
Vandana Pamulaparthy is an upcoming poet from Telangana, India. She holds a post-graduate degree in Pharmaceutics; she worked as an assistant professor in Pharmaceutical sciences before settling as a stay-at-home mother of two wonderful kids. Writing is a passion she discovered from an early age. Her poems are mostly based on emotions, relationships or just random musings as a part of her imagination. Her poems have been published in six Indian anthologies and an International anthology. She also has published a solo book of her poems called 'Dreams & Destiny'. Find her on Instagram @alittlebitof_poetry

Victoria Jay
Victoria, or as she writes under the pseudonym J.V. Dazed, has always been drawn to words and the darker things in life. A harmonious blend of both pessimist and optimist, she sees things for what they are (a realist if you may) and chooses to express herself through words and art as she has done since she was a child. Her mind has a way of its own but through creation she finds her peace.

Wilder Rose
Wilder Rose is a vivid writer of sensual and romantic words. She has been writing for over fifteen years. Rose typically writes every day on her social media platforms. Writing has always been her passion. She published her first collection of poems. "In the West Wing."

When she is not writing, she works as a genealogist librarian. She is dedicated to archival books, hunting dead people and researching her city's wild west history.

Willandria Jackson
Willandria Jackson is a poet. She enjoys inspiring others through her work, based off real life experiences. She embraces all life has to offer while striving for greatness. "Never Give Up" You can find more of Willandria's work on Instagram @willandriaspoetry

Xan Indigo
Xan Indigo is a rogue astrophysicist with an overactive imagination and a mixed up ethnic background. They mostly spend their spare time drinking too much tea, cooking spicy things, mixing cocktails, and attempting to turn their apartment into a tiny rainforest.

Zuzana Gmucova
pieces_of_zuzi, also known as Zuzi, is an artist born on August 29, 1981 in Slovakia where she grew up, studied, and lived. Poetry was a part of her life since a teenage. She started to devote herself to active creation about a year ago. She draws inspiration for writing from something that boils inside her. As she says, it's a way to process and release all kinds of feelings and emotions. Her muses are all sides of life, human dreams and nature. Her poems are raw, tender, with high dose of visualization in which she combines imagination with abstraction.

Printed in Great Britain
by Amazon

20458398R00244